W9-DJQ-944

All Roads Lead to
the American City

MAY, 2007

DEAR DAVID,
WITH FOND WISHES,

P↓√E

This publication is made possible with the support of
the U.S. Consulate General Hong Kong & Macau,
and the M.V. Dimič Research Institute,
University of Alberta, Edmonton.

All Roads Lead to
the American City

Edited by
Peter Swirski

香港大學出版社
HONG KONG UNIVERSITY PRESS

Hong Kong University Press
14/F Hing Wai Centre
7 Tin Wan Praya Road
Aberdeen
Hong Kong

© Hong Kong University Press 2007

ISBN 978-962-209-862-6 (hardback)
        978-962-209-863-3 (paperback)

All rights reserved. No portion of this publication may be reproduced or transmitted in any form or by any means, electronic or mechanical, including photocopy, recording, or any information storage or retrieval system, without permission in writing from the publisher.

Secure On-line Ordering
http://www.hkupress.org

British Library Cataloguing-in-Publication Data
A catalogue record for this book is available from the British Library.

Printed and bound by Kings Time Printing Press Ltd., in Hong Kong, China

This book is dedicated to
Faye Wong, Selina Lai,
and other students and seekers

Contents

INTRODUCTION

American City or Global Village?

Peter Swirski

Cities, for the most part, *are* America. Their values and problems define not only what the United States is, but what other nations perceive the United States to be. They are the tone-setters and pace-setters for the country and the continent, if not the entire world. Roads, on the other hand, and their impact on the American culture and lifestyle, form not only the integral part of the historical rise-and-shine of the modern city but a physical release from and a cultural antidote to its pressure-cooker stresses. Tracing the boundless variety and complexity of these twin themes, *All Roads Lead to the American City* is built around a series of interdisciplinary, intercultural, and inter-linked essays on the urban culture in America. Juxtaposing the city and the road, it looks alternatively at cities as historical, geographical, social and cultural centers of life in the land, and at roads as physical as well as metaphorical arteries that lead in and out of the city.

Whether in the Americas, Eurasia or Australasia, cities of today crawl with millions of human ants, drawn or driven there by reasons of lifestyle, employment, or internal and foreign immigration. In many sprawling conurbations, from New York City to Mexico City, their numbers already reach teens of millions; in some cities of today and the rising cities of the future—exemplified by the architectural and social blueprints for Tokyo's one *kilometer*-high Sky Cities—even tens of millions. Little wonder that behind walls of steel, concrete, brick and glass, arranged into a seemingly impenetrable architectural forest, cities of the year 2007 often look—and behave—as if spat out from a giant environmental trash compactor.

But no matter how compressed, even in their cores, cities are not solid. Beehives of habitation are crisscrossed by tendrils of traffic-bearing arteries, connective tissues of the city. Streets, roads, alleys, lanes, courts, drives, crescents, avenues, promenades, boulevards, throughways, freeways and highways—together with other open spaces such as squares, plazas, markets and parks—comprise in many cities an astonishing one-fifth of their entire size. In a car-crazy megalopolis like Los Angeles, roads and highways that crisscross it in all directions add up to no less than a quarter of its total area. And in a car-crazy country like the United States, roads and highways add up to no less than national conduits for escape from industrial nightmare and toward fulfillment of personal dreams.

In the year 1800, not too distant from the country's birth, only 6 percent of Americans lived in cities. Reflecting the new nation's history—when agriculture was king and the Jeffersonian ideal of countrified gentry pursuing "happy mediocrity" still alive—cities of the era were agglomerations of four thousand people or more. Nowadays, reflecting the marginalization of farm life and the homogenization of urban ethos throughout the land, cities are defined by the Census Bureau as settlements of 2,500 inhabitants or more. Even more to the point, the percentage of Americans living in them has crept well above 80 percent.

As a center of economic growth, political power, and cultural diversity, the city has always occupied a crucial place in America's vision of itself as a nation. Thomas Wolfe's haunting evocation of "a cruel city, but … a lovely one, a savage city, yet it had such tenderness" (473), captures well the ambivalence many have felt towards it. Examining the history, cinema, literature, cultural myths and social geography of the United States, *All Roads Lead to the American City* puts some of the greatest as well as the "baddest" American metropolises under the microscope. Examining the role of the roads that crisscross and connect the cities, it looks for ways to understand the people who live, commute, work, create, govern, commit crime and conduct business in them.

"New York is simply a distillation of the United States, the most of everything, the conclusive proof that there is an American civilization." Few words capture the dual nature of the country's (and arguably the world's) greatest metropolis as aptly as those of industrial designer, Raymond F. Loewy. They epitomize not only the socio-cultural but the geo-political mystique of the American city as a place where fortunes and lives are made or lost. For better or worse, in literature and in real life, the American urban experience is epitomized by NYC, and little wonder that this global city looms large in the chapters that follow. It has lost nothing of its dual nature, let alone its demographic and cultural prominence, since Loewy's times. It still effortlessly combines *Big Bad City* woes with the glittering *Big Lights, Big City* façade. It continues to be the final destination for many who go on the road to seek a better future, and end up in a snarled and snarling traffic nightmare.

Yet, unlike Robert Moses, who saw the bustling immigrant communities of New York only as traffic impediments, a new generation of city planners today work to turn streets into a glue that binds individual blocks and entire neighborhoods from within. The variability and complexity of American cities can be traced, of course, to the historical, demographic, and socio-cultural metamorphoses wrought in the country since its inception, and vastly accelerated during the postwar years. But these metamorphoses, in reality, are now global in nature. Identifying and investigating the disparate elements of American urban culture, the chapters below identify and investigate much of the urban culture worldwide.

Globalization is more than watching Hollywood remakes of French movies in theatres in Hong Kong, watching Nigerian footballers wearing Taiwanese-made Nikes compete in the British football leagues, or watching Algerian auto-racers using Bosch tools to fix their stalled Subarus in the Sahel. Globalization has penetrated the urban arena as well. The historical trends and cultural movements identified in *All Roads Lead to the American City* grab headlines all over the world, from São Paulo to Singapore to Sydney. Australia, in fact, may be the best case in point, with just *five* cities (Sydney, Melbourne, Brisbane, Perth and Adelaide) containing almost 60 percent of the population of the entire continent. But it's no different in Asia, home to the largest number of people living in the country but also, soberingly, the largest number of people living in the city.

China alone underlies the worldwide domination and homogenization of the urban milieu. As Jared Diamond reported in *Collapse: How Societies Choose to Fail or Succeed*, between 1953 and 2001 the country's population only doubled, but the percentage of its city dwellers *tripled* to almost 40 percent, giving the world a staggering number of more than half a billion Chinese "city-zens". In the same blink of an eye the total number of cities in China grew by 500 percent, while the existing ones swelled enormously in area. Naturally, you cannot swell an already large body without enlarging the existing arteries, whether they carry hemoglobin or people and produce. It comes as no surprise, therefore, that China's transportation network has grown faster than Yao Ming in his youth. Between 1952 and 1997, the length of railroads and motor roads leading into and out of the city has increased by 250 and 1,000 percent respectively. In one generation between 1980 and 2001, the number of non-passenger motor vehicles has increased 15-fold, and cars 108-fold!

If this sounds all too familiar, the truth is that today's global village looks more and more like the American city. Take the train from Narita through Chiba to Tokyo. Drive through the Pudong section of Shanghai. Bus across Kowloon in Hong Kong. Get on the road from Linkou to Taipei. Drearily, you'll see the same rows of concrete boxes housing the same chains of restaurants, convenience stores, night clubs, cinemas and shopping malls. Proudly advertising local businesses with English-sounding names, luring global villagers with neon promises from Toys R Us, 7–11 or Starbucks, it is sometimes hard to tell rush-hour Asia from (sub)urban USA. Where for Jack Kerouac and the Beat generation getting on the road meant escape from the conformity and uniformity of suburban existence, the McDonald-ization of culture has reached proportions undreamed of even half-a-century ago. And for all the talk of America's love affair with the automobile, even that may be a casualty of the homogenization of interstate travel. "Most of us aren't in love with the car," rues Justin Fox on the pages of *Fortune* 2004; "we're stuck in a long and passionless marriage from which there appears to be no possibility of release" (84).

The contemporary American metropolis evokes a myriad of globally recognizable images. On the one hand there is the glitter of resplendent office towers, convention and/or cultural centers, the sprawling shopping malls and cellphone-toting affluence. On the other hand there is the despair of street crime, drug addiction, failed education, homelessness and poverty. But even these contrasting pictures, no matter how rank and real, fail to reveal the whole picture of today's metropolitan life. We need research integrated across the *entire* spectrum of the humanities and social sciences to evaluate the transformations currently underway, if we are to understand where *Urbs Americana*, and with it *Urbs Asiana, Australiana, Europeana*, and even *Africana* are headed.

Hence the book in your hands.

Reflecting the variety and complexity of contemporary urban American culture, the assortment of essays and contributors is remarkably interdisciplinary, as befits the American Studies standards. The opening chapter by a historian segues into a socio-cultural analysis from a film scholar; a socio-literary essay is followed by an anatomy of American myths from a professor of religion and culture studies; all capped by a socio-demographic portrait of the United States from a geographer. Alternating in focus from the American city to the American road, the chapters pick up the various leitmotifs that animate the book: city life, its historical trends and the uneasy present, ethnic tensions in a search for national and personal identity, the tattered state of the American dream, and the constant efforts at its renewal. Combining into a constellation of cultural lenses, the experts employ a mosaic of voices, styles and approaches that mimics the richness of voices in American urban culture to bear on a wide sweep of its social history.

All Roads Lead to the American City opens with an essay by a historian, Priscilla Roberts. Panoramic in dimensions, "All Roads Lead from the American City? The Land of the Urban Frontier" traces in exquisite detail the rise of cities and urban culture in America. Distinct in its provocative inversion of the book's central thesis, it brings a consistently political perspective to bear on the volatile debates surrounding the American city. A more intimate view of the road and the road movie is offered in the second chapter, "In the City and on the Road in Asian American film: *My America … or Honk if you Love Buddha*." Gina Marchetti, a film scholar, travels in the footsteps of an Asian American filmmaker who records her first-hand experience of traversing the territory in search of her own and her country's identity.

The twin protagonists of the central chapter, "A Is for American, B Is for Bad, C Is for City: Ed McBain and the ABC of Police and Urban Procedurals," are the late master of urban fiction, Ed McBain, and New York City. With an eye towards McBain's documentary aesthetics, literature scholar Peter Swirski evaluates the literary, historical and socio-urban acumen of popular fiction about the city.

Chapter 4 provides a literary-cultural perspective by a literary and religious comparativist, Earle Waugh. Stretching from Cotton Mather to Hunter S. Thompson, "*Just Apassin' Through*: Betterment and Its Discontents in America's Literature of the Road" takes multicultural stock of American road myths and dreams that have lingered from colonial times to this day.

Motivated, much as all the preceding essays, by the unease about the human condition in urban society, William John Kyle's essay "*Urbs Americana*—A Work in Progress" concludes the collection. Replete with fact and image, it is a fitting closure inasmuch as it revisits the themes that animate it throughout: historical settlement, continental expansion, immigration and employment patterns, urban plight and flight, and efforts at renewing the American city and its human resources. No less fittingly, it concludes the analysis of American urban culture with a rare glance into what the future may hold. It would be presumptuous to claim that even the encyclopedic detail and cross-disciplinary range of studies assembled in *All Roads Lead to the American City* can exhaust the cultural gamut of America's cities and roads. But, as the adage goes, even the longest journey starts with just one step.

CHAPTER 1

All Roads Lead from the American City?

THE LAND OF THE URBAN FRONTIER

Priscilla Roberts

In Europe, picaresque accounts of travel, adventure, and self-discovery are nothing new, their models dating back to Miguel Cervantes's *Don Quixote* and the tales of Henry Fielding and Tobias Smollett, if not to *The Canterbury Tales* or *The Odyssey*. But in the popular imagination it is the United States that is the urban nation *par excellence*. According to received wisdom, it is a country of huge and impersonal concrete jungle cities, tower blocks and housing projects, linked by a network of highways along which Americans, propelled by cheap gasoline, career in huge, gas-guzzling automobiles.

In the twentieth century, the United States created not just its own brand of the road narrative, but also that distinctive genre, the road movie. Its destination was sometimes violent death, sometimes disillusionment, and occasionally a new life in the big cities that had become the great American cultural centers. Yet it may not be too far-fetched to suggest that the archetypal Hollywood seeker is Dorothy, following the yellow brick road to the Emerald City of the Land of Oz. There she learns that the feared and fabled wizard is merely an ordinary man whose tricks rely on smoke and mirrors, and there is no place like home, back on a Kansas farm with her family, while her odd assortment of companions find within themselves the qualities they once believed they lacked.

Ambivalence toward the city and its opportunities, a constant throughout American history, is implicit in much twentieth-century thinking and in demographic patterns. This was demonstrated perhaps most spectacularly in the presidential elections of 2000 and 2004, when the country found itself near evenly divided between blue (or "metro") and red (or "retro") America. The former was made out of predominantly urban states on the east and west coasts, heavily stratified by class and dominated by cosmopolitan liberal professionals, plus the country's embattled working poor. The "retro America" comprised the largely suburban or small-town areas of the South and West, heartland of the conservative middle class. In voting twice for George W. Bush, many Americans had, it seemed, rejected big-city sophistication and embraced evangelical religion and small-town, backward-looking values.

Michael Lind, political commentator and biographer of George W. Bush, even argued recently that many Americans had never found the city attractive. This iconoclastic academic, who broke with conventional wisdom by defending the Vietnam War, contended: "The American dream is a big backyard, individual bedrooms for the kids and a couple of cars—not a tiny urban apartment and a subway fare." Lind further suggested that many Americans had effectively bypassed the urban experience since outside the metropolitan northeast, "most American families have moved directly to suburbs from farms, ranches and small towns, without ever going through an urban phase." Accordingly, many recent immigrants have replicated this journey, as "Latinos and Asians go from farms and small towns abroad directly to semi-rural suburbs in the US without stopping for a generation or two in big cities."[1]

Lind's analysis suggests that patterns of immigration in the United States have changed dramatically from those a century earlier, when the big cities were the destination of choice of many immigrants, whether from overseas or internal migrants. Have they, perhaps, returned to older norms, and is the United States leading the world on the pioneering pathway to a post-urban future? Or is the American experience, as the longstanding exceptionalist tradition contends, *sui generis*?

Americans and the City: A Perennial Ambivalence

Conflicting emotions toward the attractive but dangerous opportunities urban life potentially offered have been a virtual constant in North American history. The original colonies of the seventeenth and eighteenth centuries were, like the rest of the world at that time, predominantly rural. Their cities were primarily ports, through which people and manufactured goods could enter the continent, and administrative and political centers. At the time of the revolution the population of New York, the largest American city, was probably less than 22,000, while only one individual in twenty lived in a town or city of more than 2,500 people.[2] The United States lagged behind Europe in terms of urbanization. In early nineteenth-century Europe, 13 percent of the population resided in cities with 5,000 or more inhabitants, whereas only 3.4 percent of those living in the United States did so.[3] The Puritan John Winthrop, one of the founders of Massachusetts colony, stated in 1630 that the new settlement should be "as a City upon a Hill," a near perfect society the light of whose virtue would be visible to all from afar. The model city he envisaged almost certainly resembled the traditional walled settlement common in medieval Europe and other continents—small, confined, and effectively a fortress against outside enemies. But both Boston, which he founded, and other American cities would develop on very different lines.[4]

Soon, too, at least some prominent Americans found disturbing the prospect that their country would produce great cities. One of the nation's greatest founding fathers and intellectual forebears, Thomas Jefferson, specifically tied his country's continuing success as a republic—the "great experiment" that differentiated it as a state from the hierarchical, dynastic nations of Europe—to its continuation as a democracy of relatively equal agriculturalists, fearing that its evolution into a plutocracy would inevitably create a new aristocracy. The emergence of large urban centers might also, Jefferson feared, undercut republican virtue and promote vice of every kind.

Writing to James Madison in 1787, as the assorted states gradually ratified the constitution, Jefferson stated: "I think our governments will remain virtuous for many centuries; as long as there shall be vacant lands in any part of America. When they get piled upon one another in large cities, as in Europe, they will become corrupt as in Europe."[5] He also viewed cities as haunts of the dispossessed, who could easily, as the behavior of "the *canaille* of the cities of Europe" all too often demonstrated, threaten social stability.[6] "The mobs of the great cities," he warned earlier on in 1782, "add just so much to the support of pure government as sores do the strength of the human body."[7] Jefferson's views on the nationally, morally, and politically salubrious impact of widespread cultivation of the soil or a relatively modest engagement in commerce or industry, and the deleterious effects of urban life, remained unchanged by high office. As president, in 1803 he told one correspondent: "The general desire of men to live by their heads rather than their hands, and the strong allurements of great cities to those who have any turn for dissipation, threaten to make them here, as in Europe, the sinks of voluntary misery."[8]

Until at least the mid-nineteenth century and the end of the Civil War, Jefferson's concerns seemed exaggerated, as the United States remained primarily rural. Settlers in their millions poured into the North American continent, the majority of them seeking their fortune not in the seaboard cities but by following Horace Greeley's adage "Go West, young man" (or woman). They were drawn by the lure of free or cheap land and the opportunity of becoming self-sufficient farmers, or, if professionals, of settling in small towns that effectively serviced local agriculture. They traveled, not on still often nonexistent highways, but up rivers or by overland trail, sometimes on horseback, though more often in cumbersome but serviceable covered wagons. It may be useful to remember the conclusions from a late twentieth-century biography of Austin Dickinson—brother of the poet Emily, a post-Civil War mainstay of Amherst College, Massachusetts, famous primarily for his relationship to his sister and also for his unconventional long-term adulterous liaison with a married woman. The book suggests that in the mid-nineteenth century only the least enterprising, or those with family or community ties they could not break, stayed behind in the East, missing the expansive opportunities for success and wealth accessible to those who moved west.[9]

As every textbook on the period emphasizes, the later nineteenth and early twentieth centuries—the so-called Gilded Age and Progressive Era—were a period of massive industrialization, urbanization, and immigration, which drastically changed the socio-demographic and political face of the United States. From 1860 to 1920 the number of Americans living in cities of 8,000 or more increased almost nine-fold, from 6.2 million to 54.3 million.[10] This period also saw the growth not just of cities, but of metropolises, urban centers of 100,000 people or more, which by 1930 would house one-quarter of the American population. By 1940 just under half, and by 1980 three-quarters, of Americans lived in metropolitan areas.[11]

Who, then, were those who, at the turn of the century, flocked to the American city, making the United States not just the greatest industrial power, but also apparently the most urbanized nation on earth? One can discern at least three separate groups. Fuelled by cheap steamship fares and growing popular assertiveness everywhere in Europe, immigrants from across the European continent deluged the United States in search of greater economic opportunity. Between 1865 and 1916, approximately 50 million Europeans immigrated to the United States, and increasingly they gravitated to urban centers. Despite the lure of the cities, some, especially those of Scandinavian and German extraction, still sought free or inexpensive land, and gravitated to the middle and far western agricultural states, swelling ethnically homogeneous communities of small farmers. The majority, however, increasingly flocked into the burgeoning industrial cities of the northeastern and midwestern states, providing the labor force for the manufacturing boom that soon propelled the United States into the role of potential world power, and creating an American industrial working class. In 1890, approximately 62 percent of Americans born outside the United States lived in urban centers, something that was true of only 26 percent of native-born whites with native-born parents.[12]

Urban numbers were boosted further by those native-born Americans who chose to seek their fortunes in the big cities, responding in part to high (though declining) birthrates in the late nineteenth century, reinforced by declining mortality and longer life expectancy. The mechanization of agriculture and the high cost of machinery impelled many small American farmers to desert the land for the cities. In various states, notably New Hampshire, New York, Maryland, Ohio, and Illinois, the rural population declined from the 1880s onward, with emigrants leaving the country for both well-established regional cities—among them Atlanta, Los Angeles, San Francisco, and Seattle—and newer centers, including Birmingham, Houston, Kansas City, and Albuquerque. Among those internal migrants to the cities were both African-Americans and single women.[13]

For at least a century, moreover, many intelligent young men and women found irresistibly alluring the bright lights, intellectual ferment, and cultural and career prospects of the great urban centers. The city was the place to seek one's fortune, change the world, or both. Thus from the late nineteenth century onward, patterns of opportunity and ambition began to reverse. As the ever expanding network of railroads knitted the country together, bright young people with a future flocked for the most part eastward in ever increasing numbers, to exploit the opportunities available to them in the new cities, working for and simultaneously molding business, government, academia, or the media. Future Supreme Court Justice William O. Douglas, originally from Washington State, who took this route in the 1920s, even entitled his autobiography *Go East Young Man.* Intellectuals and artists likewise found the big cities served as cultural centers offering scope for their talents.

The cities gave rise to many of the dilemmas, finding solutions for which would form the American political agenda for most of the twentieth century: the management of a large-scale industrial economy; the provision of social welfare facilities, including public housing, affordable mass transit, such essential services as sewage, gas, water, and electricity, and healthcare; how to handle mass unemployment and the care of the elderly; and the bureaucratic administration of a mass society. Although such well-established institutions as Harvard and Yale played their part, especially in legal thinking, it was *par excellence* the rising new urban universities, such as Columbia, New York University, Johns Hopkins, Pennsylvania, Chicago, and Michigan, together with progressive Wisconsin, that furnished a base for a new brand of iconoclastic intellectuals. Thomas E. Dewey, William James, Robert Hale, Lester Ward, Richard Ely, Simon Patten, and Charles Beard challenged and critiqued accepted thinking and mores, founding and developing the new social science disciplines of sociology, political science, and economics, and on occasion advised politicians.[14]

Urbanized American intellectuals and reformers soon developed close links with counterparts in West European countries, especially Great Britain, and each learnt from the other.[15] Urban experiences persuaded assorted late nineteenth-century Protestant clergymen, among them Walter Rauschenbusch of New York and Washington Gladden of Columbus, Ohio, that Christian ethics required the relatively well-off to minister actively to the needs of the poor, prompting them to found the influential Social Gospel religious movement.[16] The cities also gave rise to the settlement houses, usually staffed at least partly by idealistic young middle-class men and women. Some among these—notably Jane Addams of Chicago's Hull House, and Florence Kelley and Lillian Wald of New York's Henry Street Settlement—made a lifelong career of social work and became committed social and political activists. In general a very high proportion of those turn-of-the-century American reformers who termed themselves progressives had served at least briefly in a settlement house.[17]

Yet, whatever their magnetic attractions, among large portions of the United States population suspicions of cities remained intense. In 1920, the announcement from the National Census Bureau that more than half the

American population now lived in communities with a population over 2,500 (the official definition of a city) provoked considerable national soul-searching.[18] The impending urbanization of the United States had been presaged thirty years earlier by the National Census Bureau's declaration that the American frontier was now closed. This was, indeed, one reason for the enormous popularity of Wisconsin historian Frederick Jackson Turner's work on the frontier's impact on the American national character.[19] Cities were widely perceived as volatile haunts of disorder and social instability. As industrial turmoil and strife became features of American life, in 1877 a major railroad strike triggered riots in many United States cities, a pattern repeated in 1894, when a second national railroad strike caused President Grover Cleveland to call out the military, while unrest once again swept numerous cities.[20] Race riots, attacks on labor leaders, small businessmen, and farmers, and violence against recent immigrants, including Italians, Mexicans, and Chinese, flared up sporadically in many cities in the fifty years after the Civil War ended.[21]

Late nineteenth-century American farmers viewed the big city with a complex mixture of awe, fascination, suspicion, and distrust.[22] The agrarian Populist politician and Democratic presidential nominee William Jennings Bryan proclaimed in 1896: "[T]he great cities rest upon our broad and fertile prairies. Burn down your cities and leave our farms, and your cities will spring up again as if by magic; but destroy our farms and the grass will grow in the streets of every city in the country."[23] To Bryan, the cities were home to ever more powerful business corporations, whom he and many of his followers blamed for what they saw as major political and social defects in their nation, including a growing absence of democracy. To all appearances, Bryan was railing futilely against the prevailing trends of his time and the future. Four times a presidential candidate, he never won election to that office, and his term as Secretary of State under Woodrow Wilson ended in 1915 in ignominious resignation, due to disagreements over United States neutrality toward World War I. It was perhaps symbolic that, at the end of his life, during the 1920s Bryan would very publicly lead efforts to ban the teaching of Darwin's theory of evolution in American high schools. One may plausibly interpret this opposition to Darwinism as an exercise in cultural politics to force a modernizing country to respect the more straightforward values of an older, rural America.

Yet Bryan was by no means alone in his suspicions of the city, nor were they confined to the unsophisticated. Numerous individuals and community leaders, some prominent, others obscure, expressed fears that the closing of the frontier implied the end of the sturdy American spirit of self-reliance, individualism, and physical hardihood. Like many from the Eastern elite, Theodore Roosevelt, in some respects the first modern president, who sought to wrestle with the dilemmas of a large-scale, urban, industrial society, looked beyond the city for basic American values. After the sudden death of his youthful first wife, this rising New York politician retreated to the Far West, spending several years as a rancher in the remote Dakota "bad lands."[24] Roosevelt exulted in the experience, enjoying frequent physically demanding hunting trips in the wilderness, on which he "felt as absolutely free as a man could feel," and proclaiming, "Cowboys are a jolly set."[25]

The classic figure of the cowboy as the epitome of American national values—celebrated by him in his 1888 book *Ranch Life and the Hunting Trail*—loomed large in Roosevelt's vision of the United States. He christened the cavalry regiment he raised to fight in the Spanish-American War "The Rough Riders," both then and in the account he subsequently published, reveling in and romanticizing his rather brief experience of danger and physical combat.[26] Roosevelt's bestselling history of the early United States, *The Winning of the West* (1889–96), eulogized the centrality of the frontier experience in making the country. As president, Roosevelt not only proclaimed the therapeutic and moral value of "the strenuous life" and vigorous physical exercise, preferably in untamed natural surroundings and somewhat dangerous conditions, but was also the most prominent founder of the modern conservation movement, designed to preserve the American wilderness and the frontier experience for the benefit of future generations.[27]

Another of Roosevelt's prominent concerns was that "old stock" Americans were bearing too few children, leading to "race suicide."[28] What he meant was that the nation's population might be swamped by what he considered less desirable, non-"Anglo-Saxon" racial elements and their progeny, which would in turn, he feared, affect the country's ability to compete vigorously in the international arena, something he considered essential to national greatness. Many other old-stock Americans displayed edgy suspicion toward the new big-city immigrants, whose growing political dominance of the urban political machines they considered detrimental to American values.[29]

In 1915 Willard Straight, a young diplomat and banker close to Roosevelt, warned that heavy recent immigration meant that "our national life has been diluted by an influx of many who are strange to the fundamental aspirations which have been the finest thing in our history," and that Americans were consequently "groping" for a sense of national identity. Such sentiments fueled the early twentieth-century movement to "Americanize" immigrants and were also one important factor impelling the World War I crusade to introduce universal military training. Straight and others like him hoped that the preparedness movement would not only boost American defenses, but attain total social and spiritual regeneration, "with resultant benefits to public discipline."[30] Both undertakings won strong endorsement from Roosevelt, who invariably considered readiness to fight a gauge of both individual and national strength and virility, and feared that over-civilization might leave Americans effete and unable to defend themselves.[31]

Roosevelt's younger cousin Franklin, who presided over the New Deal social reform programs that not only addressed the concerns of the industrial working class but won the Democratic Party the loyalties of the big cities, shared his predecessor's views on the therapeutic impact of the great outdoors. A country squire who inherited a much-cherished family estate at Hyde Park, New York (overlooking the Hudson River), as president Roosevelt was the prime architect of the Civilian Conservation Corps. Between 1933 and 1941, this army-run government program took around 3 million young men, mostly from urban backgrounds, and set them to work on assorted conservation projects around the United States national park system. Not only, in Roosevelt's opinion, would this enterprise preserve and enhance the country's national heritage. It had the added benefit of introducing effete city-bred youth to nature and the countryside, thereby strengthening them both morally and physically.[32]

Yet, paradoxically, it was also Franklin Roosevelt who, under the stimulus of the Great Depression, oriented American politics decisively toward urban concerns, especially those of the often ethnic industrial working class. Although no American city was ever entirely dominated by one single ethnic group, or even by immigrants, from the late nineteenth century onward, the immigrant working class became increasingly prominent in urban politics, and especially active in the political machines that dominated municipal politics. For the most part, the Irish, Italians, Poles, Jews, and other hyphenated Americans who swelled the cities in the late nineteenth and early twentieth centuries gravitated to the Democratic Party. This was because, except in the South, the Republicans were—albeit with some notable exceptions, such as the LaFollette family of Wisconsin—the party of respectability and the "haves."

Demographically, in the first third of the twentieth century, across the United States the urban working class was the fastest growing segment of the population, fueled, perhaps, by the high birth rates Theodore Roosevelt found so inimical. The prohibition amendment of 1918—a measure Bryan and many of his agrarian liberal admirers strongly supported—was bitterly resented by many of the immigrant ethnic groups as an attempt by more abstemious old-stock Americans to force newcomers to conform to their own mores. Predictably, it quickly generated ferocious political contention, especially within the Democratic Party. In 1924 the Democratic convention deadlocked between the claims of the gentlemanly California lawyer William G. McAdoo, former Secretary of the Treasury and President Woodrow Wilson's son-in-law, and the less socially polished Irish Catholic New Yorker, Governor Alfred E. Smith of New York, a sworn opponent of prohibition whose theme song was "The Sidewalks of New York." Four years later, Smith gained the Democratic nomination and, though resoundingly defeated by Herbert Hoover—in part because his Catholicism and personal style repelled many respectable Americans—he nonetheless won the Democrats a majority in the urban industrial cities.[33]

The Democratic nominee of 1932, the well-bred Franklin Roosevelt, initially did less well than Smith in the nation's cities, but by the next election his policies had won over working-class loyalties quite decisively. Over its first four years, from 1933 to 1936, the somewhat unsystematic set of policies Roosevelt termed the New

Deal gradually became more radical, addressing the concerns of that "one-third of a nation" the president characterized in his 1937 Second Inaugural Address as "ill-housed, ill-clad, ill-nourished." By 1936 the Roosevelt administration had established the Public Works Administration, the Youth Administration, and the Civilian Conservation Corps, which gave public jobs or funded the studies of millions who would otherwise have been unemployed. It established the Social Security Act, providing pensions for the elderly and unemployment insurance for those who lost jobs after it was passed, and the National Labor Relations Act, which gave labor leaders in the Committee on Industrial Organization the green light to embark on mass unionization of such industries as steel and automobiles.

Noting that, in addition to their traditional southern base, the New Deal measures had won the Democrats the loyalties of the urban working class, organized labor, and African Americans, the journalist Samuel Lubell wrote:

> As a reporter in Washington I had shared the general belief that the New Deal was hastily improvised and animated by no coherent philosophy. When one translated its benefits down to the families I was interviewing in 1940, the whole Roosevelt program took on a new consistency.
>
> The depression had thrown grave strains upon lower income families ... In varied ways the New Deal eased these family strains. Through the HOLC [Home Ownership Loans Corporation] a million homes were saved. ...
>
> Into the CCC [Civilian Conservation Corps] camps went 2,750,000 sons of the cities. No longer a drain on the family larder, they even sent some money back home. Children in high school might get NYA [National Youth Administration] aid. Those who went to work usually did so in low-wage industries where the effects of the wage-hour law were most noticeable.
>
> ... Even persons who had done rather well for themselves were likely to have a less fortunate family member lower down the economic ladder being benefited by the New Deal. Old-age pensions and other aid eased the burden of having to care for parents too old to work. Instead of being dragged by family burdens, the rising generation was able to solidify its gains.[34]

Until the late 1960s, at the presidential level the urban-based Democratic political coalition remained virtually unbreakable.

The historian William O'Neill has termed the mid-twentieth century years the "American high." It might well have seemed that the world's strongest power both economically and militarily, enjoying what was in many ways a period of international hegemony not equaled again until the mid-1990s, was also the most citified society ever seen. Whereas in 1930 13.3 percent of Americans lived in cities with a population of more than 1 million, fifty years later the proportion had fallen steadily to 7.7 percent.[35] Even so, according to census figures in 1980 the great bulk of Americans, no less than three out of every four, lived in metropolitan areas of at least 100,000 people, and most of the rest resided within twenty-five miles of such an area.[36] In 1930, moreover, around 30 percent of the American population still lived on farms, and another 20 percent in rural areas and small villages. By 1980, the percentage of Americans living on farms had fallen to 3 percent, though the proportion of non-farming but non-urban residents had actually risen slightly, to 23 percent.[37]

The Suburbs Challenge Urban Dominance: The Twentieth-Century Confrontation

Undoubtedly some late twentieth-century Americans were irrevocably urban in their orientation. The feminist scholar and detective author Carolyn Heilbrun, ensconced in a sunny Manhattan West Side apartment, wrote: "Only those who love large cities and die a bit away from them (though they may cherish country vacations and travel for a month at a time) can know the slow depression that follows exile from a loved city."[38] Yet from the mid-twentieth century, and even before, many Americans rejected the city, especially the big city, in favor of suburban life. While most late twentieth-century Americans—far more, in fact, than fifty years earlier—lived what might be called metropolitan lives, for many the nature of that experience had changed. Increasingly, life in the inner cities seemed undesirable, at least when contrasted with the growing possibilities of the suburbs.

Even in the late nineteenth and early twentieth centuries, at the height of urban immigration, the poorest and most recent immigrants tended to cluster in the innermost urban districts. This pattern was perhaps accentuated since, especially by contrast with historically pedigreed European centers, the great majority of American cities were new creations whose real growth only began in the nineteenth century. Only 45 percent of European cities with a population of 100,000 or more in 1979 had possessed fewer than 10,000 residents in 1800. In the United States, by contrast, of 153 cities of at least 100,000 people in 1980, only twenty-three had even existed in 1800, and at that time a mere three of these had numbered more than 10,000 residents.[39] The recent antecedents of numerous major American cities meant that in many cases they grew up around industrial manufacturing plants, enabling workers to live in close proximity to the plants and businesses that employed them.

Descriptions of conditions in working-class areas of late nineteenth-century cities, such as *How the Other Half Lives* (1890) by the famous investigative journalist Jacob Riis, make it readily understandable why, from an early date, prudence and aesthetic considerations alike might impel the middle-class to distance itself physically and socially from their less affluent neighbors. With no provision for public housing, new immigrants were often lodged in overcrowded squalid tenements, firetraps that were also seedbeds for disease, frequently with no running water or direct light, and only very limited cooking facilities and sanitation. Numerous city streets were unpaved and many doubled as sewers and garbage receptacles. Urban factories were often equally unappealing, dark, crowded, full of dangerous and unguarded machinery, and liable to have firedoors locked to prevent employees from taking unauthorized breaks.

Many workers, especially women, did piecework at home, effectively converting what little domestic living space they possessed into a sweat shop. Hours were unregulated, and small children often worked with their parents or in factories.[40] Predictably, the poorer areas of cities were also often unsafe, as young boys formed gangs and crime, especially robbery of every kind, became common. Prostitution, gambling, and saloons were also prevalent.[41] So, too, was political corruption, eventually chronicled by such muckrakers as Lincoln Steffens, practices often indulged in by political machines that, even as they provided social welfare benefits for immigrants and the poor, also skimmed a substantial portion of city revenues for their own use.[42]

During the progressive period, numerous middle-class reformers sought both to improve the standards of government and to alleviate the ills of poverty in American cities, either through charity or municipal social reform. City administration itself often assumed much responsibility for the provision of public services.[43] Simultaneously, however, many of the middle class chose to remove themselves and their families from personal exposure to the worst of such evils. Physical mobility, the ability to move in the hope that elsewhere will prove more rewarding, has, of course, always been a pronounced feature of American life. In his classic work *Democracy in America*, whose two volumes were published in 1835 and 1840, the French aristocrat Alexis de Tocqueville wrote that an American "embraces a profession and quits it. He settles in a place from which he departs soon after to take his changing desires elsewhere."[44] Another foreign visitor wrote in 1847: "If God were to suddenly call the world to judgment He would surprise two-thirds of the American population on the road like ants."[45]

At any given time from 1870 to 1920, a survey of cities around the United States was likely to reveal that between 40 and 60 percent of families who had lived in a given city a decade earlier would have migrated elsewhere. In addition, it might reveal that many of those who moved prospered and did better for themselves in their new abodes. In the early twenty-first century, one among every five families in an American city is likely to move in a given year. A century earlier, the proportion was likely to be one of four, sometimes even one in three.[46]

From the later nineteenth century onward, such relocations were often to a convenient and attractive suburb. Although many think of suburbanization as a post-World War II development, in the larger and better established American cities its antecedents date back almost a century earlier. The growth of mass transit, the trolley car, the subway, and short-distance commuter railroads, made it possible for those other than the wealthy to live well away from where they worked. Suburban residences offered more space in terms both of the actual residential living plus a private yard, tree-lined streets, parks, and similar amenities. From at least the 1850s, then, cities began to develop associated suburbs. By the early 1870s, almost a hundred suburban developments with a total population of over

50,000 encircled Chicago, and in 1889, 133 miles of additional suburbs were incorporated into Chicago's municipal area.

New York, Boston, Richmond, Memphis, and Los Angeles—the last of which possessed only 6,000 inhabitants in 1870 but had grown to 100,000 seventeen years later, mostly through suburban development—had all by the late nineteenth century become the centers of substantial surrounding suburban belts. In late nineteenth-century New York, daily commuter trains carried thousands of middle and upper class professionals from Long Island and such exclusive suburbs as Englewood Cliffs, New Jersey, and Stamford, Connecticut. Commercial and retail centers, schools, and other public facilities, and, in some cases, employment in businesses migrated to the suburban belts, attracted by lower rents and property prices. All these developments made American cities more decentralized, in some ways resembling the European city model where, as in London, over time clusters of villages gradually agglomerated together. Cities also became more segregated and socially and economically stratified, as the middle class moved out, leaving lower income workers often trapped in the inner cities.[47]

While some suburbs remained part of (or were subsequently incorporated into) the greater metropolitan area, others incorporated themselves, effectively removing themselves from the city's tax base. In many cases this enabled them to enact their own regulations on such controversial issues as the use of alcohol, vice districts, and industrial pollution, effectively excluding these perceived social evils should their citizens so desire.[48] In some cases, notably the District of Columbia and New York City, many who still worked in the metropolitan center actually lived in another state jurisdiction, further complicating the fiscal situation, usually to the detriment of the central urban area.

Over time, suburbanization accelerated. Changes in transportation made it more convenient for the middle class to leave the cities, while those factors impelling them outward intensified. New immigrants, especially those with few economic resources to propel them further, had for decades tended to cluster in the centers of those cities where they arrived or close by, boosting the population of such port cities as Boston, New York, Philadelphia, Houston, and San Francisco. In the late nineteenth century, African Americans began to join them. From 1880 onward, economic hardship impelled black Americans to move from rural sharecroppings to southern cities. Their numbers in Memphis, for example, tripled in the following two decades and grew by no less than 600 percent in Chattanooga. By 1910 they comprised 28 percent of the southern urban population, and over 40 percent in cities such as Memphis and Birmingham.[49]

Lesser numbers went north and west, to such cities as Washington, DC where, by 1910, almost 100,000 African Americans comprised 28.5 percent of the population. Still smaller contingents emigrated to New York, Philadelphia, Chicago, Denver, Oklahoma City, Detroit, Cleveland, and Los Angeles. Even though, in most northern and western cities, blacks still amounted to less than 2 percent of the total population, the influx forced the existing black communities to expand, driving out any remaining white residents.[50]

With World War I, black migration to urban centers accelerated and continued through the following two decades, fueled first by prosperity and then by depression, which drove many black tenant farmers off the land. The effective cessation of European immigration from 1915 onward made African American labor increasingly crucial to the American industrial economy. By 1920, 30 percent of all blacks—and 80 percent of the non-southern African American population—lived in cities, an increase of 900,000 in one decade. Perhaps predictably, as the wartime influx in particular strained existing facilities and brought African American competition with immigrant whites for housing, black homes were subjected to sporadic fire bombings. Lynchings and mob attacks also took place, some escalating into race riots, notably in East St. Louis in July 1917, then in Chicago, Washington, Omaha, and eventually twenty-three other cities in the summer of 1919.[51]

The presence of African Americans sparked a resurgence of the Ku Klux Klan and its extension from the South to northern and western cities.[52] But African American numbers continued to rise, usually more than doubling in non-southern cities over the subsequent decade, and constituting between 5 and 10 percent of the population in many non-southern cities. During the 1920s the number of African Americans in New York grew from 152,000 to 328,000, in Chicago from 109,000 to 234,000, in Philadelphia from 134,000 to 220,000, in Detroit from 41,000 to 120,000, and in Cleveland from 34,000 to 72,000. Overall, during the 1920s alone northern cities absorbed over 600,000 African American migrants.[53]

The increasing prominence of African Americans in major urban centers further impelled white flight to the suburbs, as the middle class rejected the city for more congenial lifestyles and neighbors outside its bounds. So, too, did the spread of the automobile. Henry Ford, founder of the Ford Motor Company, located his factories in the suburban outskirts of Detroit and paid his workers the outstandingly high wage of $5 per day, in the expectation this would enable them to purchase the motor cars they were producing. Other car manufacturers followed suit.

In many, if not most, cases, their hopes were fulfilled. In 1900, there were only eight thousand automobiles in the United States, all of them luxury and novelty items carrying a high price tag. By 1924 at least 55,000 Americans owned automobiles, a number that soared to 134,000 by 1929.[54] The rapid extension of car ownership to the middle and even the working class in the 1920s was a boon to the rural population. It also made it possible for employees to live at some distance from both their place of work and the nearest subway or trolley station, further encouraging suburbanization and less dense housing patterns. City governments tended to invest in highways rather than mass transit, and manufacturing increasingly relocated into the suburbs, deserting the inner cities.

During the 1920s, for the first time the growth rate of the suburbs surpassed that of the cities themselves, as the areas around Chicago, Los Angeles, St. Louis, Detroit, Cleveland, New York, and other cities expanded. Some early working-class suburbs were racially and ethnically diverse, and African American suburbs emerged in various locations in Ohio, North Carolina, Illinois, New York, New Jersey, and the outskirts of Washington, DC, but for the most part suburbs were increasingly white, middle class, and ethnically homogeneous.[55] Increasingly Americans lived in metropolitan districts, comprised of a city and its suburbs, and many of them were not residents of the cities themselves. By 1930, ninety-three such areas had populations surpassing 100,000, a development that continued, with the number of metropolitan areas rising to 140 in 1940. Spreading to such previously non-urbanized areas as the Southeast, Southwest, Plains, and Mountain regions, by that time they were home to almost half the American population.[56]

As these figures suggest, the Great Depression gave merely a temporary check to the spread of the city, which accelerated again after World War II. During that conflict, just as in the 1914–18 war, black and now Latino urban migration intensified, sparking major race riots in Detroit and Los Angeles.[57] For many Americans, the postwar inner cities appeared even less desirable than their prewar counterparts. Public housing projects, funded by New Deal programs and accommodating relatively poor and often ethnically diverse families, were rarely seen as enhancing their neighbors' property values. Southern blacks continued to migrate to northern and western cities after 1945. Between 1950 and 1970, some 5 million African Americans, most from the Deep South, moved into American cities, as did Latinos and Asians.

During the same time a full 7 million whites left urban centers. City cores became disproportionately black and to some extent Latino in composition, while whites—except for those too poor to move—were largely segregated in the suburbs. Once the war was over, ever greater numbers of white Americans followed, their transit facilitated by a housing construction boom, the product in part of accumulated wartime savings and generous home loans under the GI Bill of Rights. Since the majority of blacks had access only to relatively poorly paid jobs, lived in often substandard housing, and received inadequate public services (notably health and education), by the early 1960s both the tax bases and the physical condition of the inner cities had deteriorated dramatically.[58]

High birthrates and the conventional 1950s wisdom that the ideal family consisted of four children likewise helped to propel the average American into the suburbs. All roads, it seemed, led out of the American city. Even as public transportation was starved of funds, the Eisenhower administration's 1956 Highway Act built an eventual 42,500 miles of roads, 90 percent of them constructed at federal expense. Many bore Americans and the businesses that employed them out to the suburbs and beyond. No less than $15 billion of the $27 billion of funds used for highway construction in the decade after the Act was devoted to roads in urban areas. Without a private car, life in the suburbs was often unfeasible.

Predictably, in the fifteen years after 1945, the number of automobiles in the United States rose by 133 percent.[59]

Metropolitan areas became increasingly sprawling and decentralized. A popular song suggested that suburban homes were "all built out of ticky-tacky, and they all look just the same." Sociologists, including C. Wright Mills, William Whyte, and David Riesman deplored the pressures for social conformity to which, especially in the era of Senator Joseph McCarthy and political witch-hunts, suburban dwellers were often exposed.[60] Yet in practice, a great many 1950s Americans seem to have enjoyed the suburban lifestyle.[61] Certainly, in the late twentieth century, conservatives such as Republican Congressman Newt Gingrich would look back to the 1950s as an era of stability and certainty representing a golden age of American life.

Despite renewal programs intended to revitalize downtown urban areas, in the 1950s and 1960s, the inner cities settled into a spiral of decay and hopelessness, abandoned to blacks and the hard-core poor, many of whom lived on welfare in adverse family circumstances. During the 1960s, as the civil rights movement intensified without bettering the lot of the poorest of African Americans, American cities became the haunt of such radicals as Malcolm X and Black Power activists. In the later 1960s regularly erupting racial riots devastated dozens of cities around the United States, including Los Angeles, San Francisco, Portland, New York, Boston, Newark, Cincinnati, Dayton, Cleveland, Rochester, Philadelphia, Kansas City, Omaha, Chicago, Milwaukee, Atlanta, Miami, Nashville, and even the nation's capital. No urban center, it seemed, was immune. In response, still more white Americans—and, as civil rights legislation outlawed discrimination in housing, middle-class blacks—abandoned the cities for the suburbs.[62]

Americans Shun the Big City: The Political Impact

Post-World War II conservative politicians swiftly capitalized on Middle America's determined rejection of the city. Changing demographic patterns likewise threatened traditional political alignments, especially those of the once solid South to the Democratic Party. From the 1940s onwards, southern and western "sunbelt" cities were expanding at the expense of the old "rustbelt" conurbations of the industrial northeast, where so many immigrants had flocked previously. The politically motivated distribution of wartime and then Cold War defense contracts to such areas further encouraged those regions' industrial development and population growth—as did the low-tax, anti-union policies of southern states.[63]

It was perhaps symbolic that John Steinbeck's Joad family, fleeing the midwestern dustbowl of the 1930s, eventually made their way to California, where its members no doubt profited from the World War II defense boom, finding jobs in the wartime factories and settling in the state's vast network of often much dispersed, low-rise metropolitan areas, which by 1980 housed 95 percent of

California's population.[64] Although the most urbanized of all the United States, California was only spearheading a trend. By 1970, for the first time more Americans lived in suburbs than in cities: 76 million were suburban dwellers, 64 million lived in the central cities, and an additional 60 million still remained in the non-metropolitan areas.[65]

As once working-class American families prospered, joined the middle class, and decamped to the suburbs, their loyalties to the Democratic Party became increasingly frayed. Under President Lyndon B. Johnson in the 1960s, the Democrats' endorsement of civil rights legislation lost his party the allegiance of most of the white South, once an indispensable part of the Democratic coalition. At the same time many Democrats' apparent endorsement of the counterculture and antiwar protests repelled numerous culturally conservative Americans, many from the ethnic working class, who had previously been reliable Democratic supporters.

In the 1968 presidential election, 10 million Southerners voted for the breakaway Democrat, Governor George Wallace of Alabama. Their revolt proved only a half-way house to switching to the Republican Party and voting in 1972 for Richard Nixon, who skillfully appealed to white resentment of civil rights legislation and what they perceived as the moral decay of the United States. From then onward, the Republicans were the majority party of American politics, remaining so in the twenty-first century.[66] Even Jimmy Carter and Bill Clinton, the two Democratic presidents who won election after 1968, came from relatively rural southern states, while Nixon, Ronald Reagan, George H. W. Bush, and his son George W. Bush, all had solid sunbelt California or Texas credentials. The one exception, Gerald Ford of Michigan, was an accidental president, selected primarily because of the troubles Nixon and his vice-president, Spiro Agnew, encountered due to Watergate and other scandals.

As political alignments shifted, the United States, uniquely among Western industrial and post-industrial nations, re-embraced the values of the free market and limited government. Emulated by conservatives such as the British Margaret Thatcher, the German Helmut Kohl, and the French Valéry Giscard d'Estaing, this pattern reverted to the symbolic and cultural memories of an earlier, pre-urban United States. In this, if nothing else, the late twentieth-century United States broke with its conservative West European counterparts. When Thatcher openly and self-consciously proclaimed her admiration for Victorian values, she was looking back to the standards of a globally dominant, urban, and industrial economy. Labour Prime Minister Tony Blair, while stealing and adapting many of the policies of his Conservative predecessors, likewise embraced the values of an urban multicultural society, banning the traditional country pursuit of foxhunting, and showed little empathy for agriculture. Blair's lack of interest in the damage that foot-and-mouth disease wreaked on British farming communities in 2001 even attracted implicit criticism from the heir to the throne, Prince Charles, himself widely considered far less attuned to the concerns of inner-city groups than his charismatic late wife, Diana.

By contrast, Richard Nixon and perhaps Gerald Ford and George H. W. Bush were the last American presidents who felt free to present themselves as the products of an urban nation and were comfortable in doing so. Even Nixon's two Democratic predecessors both paid tribute to their country's emotional heritage. John F. Kennedy of Massachusetts, perhaps the most urban of all twentieth-century presidents, christened his admittedly limited reform program the "New Frontier" and, despite—or perhaps because of—horrendous personal health problems, ironically emulated Theodore Roosevelt in his emphasis on individual physical vigor and fitness and national virility.[67] After many years as a superlative Washington political fixer and manipulator, his successor, Lyndon Johnson—who when young had, it is true, occasionally done farm labor—sported cowboy hats and roughhewn manners and gloried in his Texas ranch.

From the 1970s onward, some kind of rural or quasi-rural background became virtually *de rigueur* for American presidents, the late twentieth-century substitute for the conventional nineteenth-century log cabin birthplace. Jimmy Carter was in most respects a Georgia hayseed, not always an asset in his presidency. The highly intelligent and charming (though less than reliable) chameleon Bill Clinton hailed from rural Arkansas but, after studying at Yale and Oxford, could be all things to all men and indeed all women, switching from southern old boy to New York sophisticate when he thought it appropriate. Vaunted Texas background and fondness for hurling horseshoes notwithstanding, few regarded the first George Bush, son of a New York investment banker, as a country boy, something two of his earlier twentieth-century Republican predecessors, Herbert Hoover and Dwight D. Eisenhower, genuinely were.

More interesting, perhaps, are the cases of Ronald Reagan and George W. Bush. Reagan came from an extremely small town in Illinois but spent many years in the celluloid city of Hollywood, before working as a front man for General Motors. Reagan presented himself, however, as a modern cowboy, as president spending all his spare time horse-riding and chopping wood on his California ranch, a pattern largely emulated—except, perhaps, for the horse—by the Texan George W. Bush. Each appealed to the symbols of an earlier American past and—despite having deftly avoided military service in combat—a gun-toting frontier heritage that dwellers in the new suburbs of the South and West clearly found attractive. They portrayed Americans as fearless and individualist gunslingers who, in their modern incarnation, needed ready access to semi-automatic weapons and heavily armored if gas-guzzling SUVs to cope with and confront the stresses of modern suburban frontier life, an outlook they expected a sympathetic and decidedly right-wing God to endorse.[68]

In California in 2003, a similar image propelled into the governorship the athletic Hollywood star, Arnold Schwarzenegger, famed mainly for playing muscle-bound action heroes such as Conan the Barbarian. From there was not far to Rambo, another film figure who took on, and through sheer physical strength and fitness overcame, longtime enemies of the United States in still culturally contentious Vietnam, purportedly liberating American MIAs whom "deceptive" Vietnamese officials had not returned. On the international scene, Reagan and Bush each purveyed an image of the United States itself as a nation ready, perhaps even eager, to employ military force regardless of the risk of war with its enemies, a country whose primary measures of global strength were its arsenals of technologically advanced weaponry and their superiority to those of any potential opponents.[69]

Rejection and suspicion of the urban was nothing new. Many Americans have always viewed their country's big cities as the incubator of dangerous forces—be they subversive political radicalism, hostile and alien immigrants, sexual nonconformity, questionable movies and music, or incomprehensible and sometimes blasphemous modern art—that actively seek to undermine traditional American values. Efforts at censorship were one response. In 1999 New York Mayor Rudolf Giuliani supported moves to close a publicly funded exhibition in Brooklyn of art works belonging to the noted collector and advertising executive Charles Saatchi that included pieces hostile critics alleged were both violent and blasphemous, condemning them for denigrating Christian beliefs by juxtaposing elephant dung and representations of the Virgin Mary. This episode represented only one of numerous efforts by cultural conservatives in the 1980s and 1990s to deny federal and other government funding to such undertakings as an exhibition of homoerotic photographs by Robert Mapplethorpe, and in some cases to re-classify them as pornography.

Concurrently, political figures and social activists—some from such predominantly right-wing groups as the Moral Majority but others, such as Democratic Vice-President Al Gore's wife Tipper, by no means politically conservative—spearheaded moves to sanitize the content of rock music and television programs, and to prevent young people from gaining Internet access to pornographic and other morally questionable websites. Such fears of the detrimental cultural impact of modernity on broad societal health were nothing new. The 1913 Armory International Exhibition of Modern Art in New York created a public furor, as contemporary pundits attacked its array of Abstract Expressionist, Cubist, Impressionist, Ashcan School, and other works for being so disturbing, both as to subject matter and technique, that they were potentially subversive of public order, morality, and decency, threatening overall social stability. So, too, in the opinion of many commentators, were the bohemian and *ipso facto* decadent lifestyles of many of the American artists whose works were represented in the Armory Show, or who admired its exhibits.

It was often far from easy to discern the boundaries between cultural nonconformity and outright political threat to American society. Throughout the twentieth century, conservatives frequently perceived their country's great cities as the primary breeding grounds and shelters for "un-American" forces, political as well as social, effectively excluding the urban nation from the "real" America. The 1919 anti-radical "Red Scare" focused on purportedly alien and generally city-dwelling subversives, several thousand of whom, born outside the United States, were deported. New Deal leftists, again generally urban-based and often working for the new federal government agencies, were the primary target of the House Un-American Activities Committee established in 1938. In the 1950s, McCarthyites accused both political and social nonconformists of undermining the American way of life and thereby weakening their country's capacity to continue waging Cold War against the Soviet Union, whose communist ideology was likewise presented as a global threat to American values.

The counterculture of the 1960s, when radical political, social, and cultural dissent went hand in hand, generated enormous and still potent hostility among more conservative Americans. They portrayed their opponents as urban-based moral degenerates who sought to overthrow all accepted American values and hierarchies, including patriotism, religion, government, family, and morality, and whose political outlook could only be considered treasonable. A similar perspective informs the hostility of the current religious and political right, which is broadly anti-urban, anti-intellectual, and anti-elitist, deeply hostile to such putatively ungodly practices as homosexuality, abortion, and the teaching of evolution, and professedly patriotic and pro-military. Yet, at the same time, it proclaims itself suspicious of big government, especially city-based federal agencies associated with the social welfare state.

Is the United States, in the title of a popular film of the 1980s, journeying back to the future? The road movie, that quintessentially American media genre, is not necessarily a celebration of the urban. Rather, it effectively updates a far older American cultural theme, that of the man on his own, the lone ranger facing the wilderness and his own weaknesses, an archetype neatly adapted to modern mechanization, as the automobile replaced the horse and bestowed even greater mobility upon the protagonist. And roads may not only lead to but also be a means of escaping the city. It is perhaps no accident that the reputation of President Theodore Roosevelt, a muscular Christian, historian, and athlete who celebrated the American West and sought to reconcile older American values of frontier individualism and physical hardihood with a modern, urban, and industrial society, has recently soared dramatically. Republican presidential hopeful and genuine war hero, Senator John McCain, is only one of those who greatly admire him.

The continuing American rejection of the urban may also have implications for its international relations. Recently then-Defense Secretary Donald Rumsfeld and Dutch-born New York University historian Tony Judt have both, in disparate ways, suggested that the United States is very different from Western Europe—or at least, in Rumsfeld's undiplomatic wording, from "old Europe." The difference is said to be that the US is more aggressive, or at least assertive, on the international scene and more likely to act unilaterally. Judt supplemented these characteristics with the observations that the United States exhibits much greater discrepancies of wealth and poverty than European nations, and is far less committed to government intervention, social welfare programs, and international agreements.[70] As his country prepared to invade Iraq, the American academic Robert Kagan notoriously stated that, "on major strategic and international questions today, Americans are from Mars and Europeans are from Venus," words that would undoubtedly have amazed audiences a mere century earlier.[71] By the early twenty-first century, however, a US president facing intractable external challenges was clearly comfortable employing bellicose diplomatic rhetoric that drew on the frontier heritage and Western movies, and in adopting measures that often left his country isolated internationally. His electoral success suggests, however, that such tactics resonated with a substantial number of Americans.

The historian David Potter argued over fifty years ago that Americans were a "people of plenty," enjoying an abundance of resources that accounted for many of the "exceptionalist" features of United States politics and society.[72] It is tempting to enquire whether the ready availability of land for suburban development in the United States, together with the longstanding anti-urban tradition and frontier mindset, conceivably account for the persistent American rejection of the urban, multicultural, and secular society. Could these factors lie behind the continuing nostalgic efforts of the world's current superpower to recapture the values of an earlier, pre-industrial, and agrarian nation? Perhaps, but if so, this outlook may be primarily for domestic consumption rather than for export. In the international sphere, allies and opponents alike who find American rhetoric and policies unpersuasive have other options, and may well simply refuse to cooperate in such unwelcome initiatives as the invasion and stabilization of Iraq.

In the United States itself, however, appeals to anti-urban values may prove more successful. Prophesy is always risky, especially in the day when America faces an ideological challenge from Islamic forces that likewise reject many aspects of modernity. Nonetheless, given prevailing demographic trends and the apparent strength of a fairly conservative Republican Party, it seems that for the indefinite future public discourse and political maneuvering in the world's most economically developed nation will probably reflect to a surprising degree the emotional heritage and imagery of a rural frontier society looking back to an idealized past.

CHAPTER 2

In the City and on the Road in Asian American Film:

MY AMERICA ... OR, HONK IF YOU LOVE BUDDHA

Gina Marchetti

In American culture, the road and the city have many different meanings.[1] For Asian Americans, for example, the road may not open up a frontier of possibilities and hope for a broad horizon of opportunities. Rather, it may signify the ultimatum of leaving town, facing a lynch mob, or even the tragedy of the forced evacuation of the Internment during the Second World War. Similarly, the city may not signal the Puritan promise of the "city on the hill." Rather, it may mean racist exclusionism, being sequestered into ethnic ghettoes, or relying on quick wits to stay one step ahead of deportation. Likewise, the city may mean shouldering the burden of the stigma of Orientalist fantasies of Chinatown opium dens, tong wars, singsong girls, Filipino servants, Korean grocers, and Japanese spies.

Asian American writers have looked critically at both the city and the road in literature. From memoirs of students in the United States to melodramas of interracial romance, Asian American authors began to imagine America during the years leading up to World War II. Carlos Bulosan's *America Is in the Heart* (1943) recounts the story of his emigration from the Philippines and encounters with racism in the new country. Postwar Japanese Americans saw their road to a better life in America as a trail of tears, recalling forced displacement and imprisonment in books such as John Okada's *No-No Boy* (1957) and Jeanne Wakatsuki Houston and James D. Houston's *Farewell to Manzanar: A True Story of Japanese American Experience During and After the World War II Internment* (1973).

Chinese Americans also began to speak out against the racism they had to confront while building America's roads and railroads and establishing themselves in urban Chinatowns. Louis Chu's *Eat a Bowl of Tea* (1961), Frank Chin's play *The Chickencoop Chinaman* (1981), and Maxine Hong Kingston's sagas, *The Woman Warrior: Memoir of a Girlhood Among Ghosts* (1976) and *China Men* (1980), point to the different ways in which Asian immigrants see themselves as part of the history of the American city and landscape.

Popular culture, however, has painted a very different picture of Asian Americans on the road and in the city. Hollywood has portrayed them as drifters in the old West—think, for example, of David Carradine as Kwai Chang Caine in the 1972–75 *Kung Fu* television series, or David Chung as Tinman Wong in the 1993 *Ballad of Little Jo*. There were also Chinatown inhabitants of the "evil" city in pictures such as *The Tong Man* (1919), *The Hatchet Man* (1932), *Mr. Wong in Chinatown* (1939), *Year of the Dragon* (1985), and others. Typically, in many of them, even elements of the décor and costuming—shoji screens, kimonos, statues of Buddha, and other objects associated in the cinematic imagination with Asia—serve as indicators of danger, treachery, and deceit. In turn, films like *The Lady from Shanghai* (1947) and *Chinatown* (1974) use Chinatown as a backdrop, strikingly without including any Asian characters as principal players in the drama. Others, like *The Big Sleep* (1946), typical of *film noir* from the 1940s and 1950s, simply use Asian objects to create an atmosphere of mystery and foreboding.[2]

Although Chinese motifs dominate many of these "wicked city" films, others, from *The Crimson Kimono* (1959) to *Showdown in Little Tokyo* (1991), deal with urban Japanese enclaves as well as other Asian ethnic communities. Given the dominant role of Hollywood in defining Asian America for world audiences, it comes as no surprise that Asian American filmmakers should devote their attention to countering Hollywood's racist depictions on screen. Because the road and the city have been so important—both historically and cinematically—to the way in which Asian America has been imagined within the popular consciousness, a number of Asian American directors and producers have turned to the "road movie" and, even more often, the "city film" to reclaim the cultural image of Asian America outside Hollywood ignorance and prejudice.

Some movies, such as Wayne Wang's *Chan Is Missing* (1982), put their characters on the road within the city. *Chan Is Missing* features a taxi driver on the road looking for the elusive Chan of the title. However, it is also very much a city film about San Francisco, referring to Tinseltown's history of Chinatown figures like the detective Charlie Chan. In conversation with the Hollywood "road movie," Abraham Lim's *Roads and Bridges* (2001) features a character in trouble with the law, Johnson Lee (played by the filmmaker himself), who ends up serving time cleaning up trash from the side of the road in the American Midwest. Other directors have actually gone on the road in search of their family history. In *The Magical Life of Long Tak Sam* (2004), for example, Canadian filmmaker Ann Marie Fleming goes in search of her Chinese grandfather, an itinerant magician and acrobat. In films such as *Family Gathering* (Lise Yasui, 1988), *History and Memory* (Rea Tajiri, 1991), and *Memories from the Department of Amnesia* (Janet Tanaka, 1991), others have traced the footsteps of their parents and grandparents displaced by the infamous 1940s' Internment.

This, of course, is only the beginning. Asian Americans have symbolically taken back the city from Hollywood and revised the cinematic history of their urban experience through independent filmmaking. Arthur Dong's *Sewing Woman* (1983) and *Forbidden City USA.* (1989), the late Steven Ning's short *Freckled Rice* (1983), and Christine Choy's *From Spikes to Spindles* (1976), all depict American Chinatowns in ways vastly different from Orientalist Hollywood fantasies. In addition to the already mentioned *Chan Is Missing*, Wayne Wang's other films set in Chinatown—including *Dim Sum: A Little Bit of Heart* (1985), *Eat a Bowl of Tea* (1989), and *The Joy Luck Club* (1993)—have opened up American cinema to a world of romantic melodramas, generation gaps, and community struggles. One must not, of course, forget films such as Spencer Nakasako and Sokly Ny's *a.k.a Don Bonus* (1995), Ahrin Mishan and Nick Rothenberg's *Bui Doi: Life Like Dust* (1994), Nith Lacroix and Sang Thepkaysone's *Letter Back Home* (1994), or Spencer Nakasako's *Kelly Loves Tony* (1998). In their distinct ways, all have looked at the way new immigrants from Indochina have transformed the American inner city.

The Korean grocer may have by now become a fixture in movies about urban America—look no further than Spike Lee's *Do the Right Thing* (1989). Asian American filmmakers have indeed taken a closer look at African/Korean American interactions in films such as Dai Sil Kim-Gibson and Christine Choy's *Sa-I-Gu* (1993), Chris Chan Lee's *Yellow* (1998) and Michael Cho's *Another America* (1996). On the other hand, Vivek Renjen Bald's *Taxi-Vala/Auto-biography* (1994) and Allen Glazen and Shebana Coelho's *Desi: South Asians in New York* (2000) explore the world of Indians and Pakistanis in the Big Apple. Other productions have looked at the multicultural mix, no longer bounded by the urban ethnic ghetto, which has become Asian America. Quentin Lee and Justin Lin's *Shopping for Fangs* (1997), for example, moves from the urban to the suburban, and their contemporary story of young Asian Americans ends with its protagonists on the road in search of new identities within an ever-changing American landscape.

In Search of Asian America

Made in the same year as *Shopping for Fangs*, Renee Tajima-Peña's documentary *My America ... or, Honk if You Love Buddha* (1997) also takes Asian Americans on the road to reclaim the expanse of the country for its ethnic minorities. Given that the "road movie" is usually associated with young white males claiming their "natural" right to the American highway, Tajima-Peña's decision to work in this genre throws down a gauntlet to this cultural exclusion. She stakes a defiant, political claim to the road as an Asian and as a woman in the film.

Part of a documentary tradition that includes historical films, personal memoirs, portraits of community leaders, and slice-of-life stories of ordinary people, *My America* stands out for its ability to combine these staples of Asian

American filmmaking into a witty and vibrant look at both the old and the new in the community. Tajima-Peña is a celebrated documentary filmmaker whose credits include *Who Killed Vincent Chin?* (1987) and *Yellow Tale Blues: A Tale of Two American Families* (1990; both co-directed with Christine Choy).[3] Drawing on her own experiences as a pioneering director, she deftly places *My America* in conversation with a history of Asian American feature filmmaking (e.g., Wayne Wang's *Chan Is Missing,* 1982), feminist film practice ("consciousness raising" cinema), activist film and video (California and Third World Newsreel), as well as the established genre of the "road movie."[4]

Who Killed Vincent Chin? examines the case of a Chinese American man beaten to death by two whites in Detroit at the height of anti-Japanese sentiments occasioned by the downturn in the American auto industry in the 1980s. *My America* takes an equally unblinking look at race relations in the American city. In addition, like *Yellow Tale Blues: A Tale of Two American Families,* Tajima-Peña uses autobiographical elements and portraits of people within the Asian American community to examine the struggle of the United States to redefine its identity within an increasingly multicultural landscape. As the title implies, *My America* is a very personal film, based on family history, memory, and individual observation of the nation. However, when you shift attention to the subtitle, ... *Honk if You Love Buddha* promises to highlight the ironic or even comic side of the Asian American experience. *My America* moves effortlessly among the forms it cites— sometimes telling a story, at other times making a didactic point or taking a pedagogical stance regarding American history.

In *My America,* Tajima-Peña uses her journey across the United States to explore the journey of Asians in America. Her personal story and family history become benchmarks on her travels to key cities that have become home to Asian Americans. The Japanese Internment and earlier instances of racism put her parents and grandparents "on the road" against their will, and she uses this experience as the backdrop for other stories about the history of Asians in America. Traveling to New York, New Orleans, Duluth, Los Angeles, Chicago and San Francisco, among other cities, Tajima-Peña maps out the experiences of Asian Americans of various regions, generations, and national/ethnic origins. The relationship between the road and the city paints a picture of Asian American history in terms of movement and settlement, social change and tradition, stigmatization and activism. The filmmaker's odyssey takes her from Chinese businessmen to Southeast Asian refugees, from campus activists to rap singers, in a celebration of the enduring power and creative accomplishments of these communities.

The tropes of the road and the city highlight the ways in which Tajima-Peña places Asian Americans in the country's sometimes rural, sometimes urban, environment that differs greatly from—even as it parallels—the territories historically occupied by European immigrants to the New World and other ethnic groups. The history of Asians in America goes, after all, from the extremes of

Figure 2.1
Filmmaker Renee Tajima-Peña
as a child visiting the Statue of
Liberty in New York City

Figure 2.2
Renee Tajima-Peña
with Victor Wong

forced movement (Chinese "driven out of town" in the Old West or following the eastward expansion of the railroad as laborers; Japanese forced on the road because of the Internment) to enclosed settlement, with immigrants sequestered within the confines of Chinatown, Little Tokyo, Little Saigon, and other ethnic ghettos. While her "America" may resemble mainstream Hollywood depictions of the road and the city, it also shows that those concepts are relative within a United States struggling with a racist past, working within a multiracial present, and dreaming of a multicultural future.

In fact, on the road and in the city, Tajima-Peña offers the bitter with the sweet. *My America* uses a dialectical structure to position Asian American life within the broader contradictions of American culture that pit blacks against whites, the rich against the poor, the conservative against the progressive, the North against the South, men against women, and the native against the foreign born. Through her keen observation and careful editing, the director uncovers these dialectical relations that underpin the Asian American experience. The film juxtaposes, for instance, immigrants who come for economic reasons with those who seek personal freedom and the possibility of equality. Granting that leaving poverty behind often means leaving behind traditional caste or class differences, more rigid definitions of gender roles, or an oppressive (neo)colonial government, the film also highlights the enormous differences between immigrants who become multi-millionaires and those who become laborers, artists or activists.

Similarly, *My America* juxtaposes the experiences of those who cling to an Asian identity as opposed to those who strive for assimilation. Again, the roots of this opposition have a common origin. The "sojourners" in America have difficulty feeling at home in a place where they are excluded and treated as foreigners for successive generations. Yet, that same racist exclusionism also creates the need to blend in at any cost, since being "too" Asian and standing out courts disaster (from racist taunts to overt violence). Some dream of returning to a "homeland" that no longer exists, while others dream of erasing the "Asian" from "Asian American." Emerging from the Asian urban ghetto and the tokenism of the white-bread suburb, *My America* becomes a place of exclusion and assimilation, conflict and transcendence, a place of constant struggle and renewal. Even as Tajima-Peña offers a vision of a troubled past, she offers hope—if not for actual change, then the possibility for genuine change to occur.

Tajima-Peña takes full responsibility for her depiction of "my" America. In the opening minutes, she states in voice-over: "This is the story of my search for Asian America." Her words define the project. "My" indicates her singular perspective, which may be open to bias or error, but also carries the authority of her own experience and personal history. The "story" pushes the film from history to "her story," and allows her to move between the cold facts and the unvoiced truths behind the "official" account of Asians in America. Her search implies a goal, but without a certain or predetermined outcome. It indicates that something of value is indeed likely to be discovered on the trip, and the viewer becomes a travel companion to find the "place" called "Asian America".

Beginning with the question "Will we ever truly belong in America?", Tajima-Peña continues throughout the film to put Asian America in perspective by asking questions that trouble her own sense of identity and her own position on the country's "map." Key themes emerge as the film unfolds and her journey progresses, and she returns repeatedly to questions of identity (national, ethnic, regional), generation gaps and conflicts, class hierarchies and economic issues, marriage and sexuality, racism and the Civil Rights movement. She reminisces about taking road trips with her family as a child growing up in the 1950s–60s, and seeing no Asian faces for miles. Now, she notes, Asian Americans are "all over the map." However, as becomes clear during the scenes when she tunes into a talk-show on her car radio, racism persists as the callers give voice to their ignorance of Asian Americans.

Of course, the question of belonging extends far beyond the white, bourgeois, Anglo-American community. An anonymous female caller, for example, calls Asian Americans "prejudiced and arrogant people—show their true colors with black people." The positioning of Asian Americans between blacks and whites becomes, in fact, a major theme in the film.[5] Later on, Tajima-Peña will revise her own question: "What have we given back [after the Civil Rights Movement]?" Broadening her query even further, she will note: "I began this journey searching for Asian America, but I realize I am also searching for America." Visually referencing the Oklahoma City bombing (1995) by showing a multicultural mix of victims and rescuers, the filmmaker begins to revise her definition of the American people. She concludes with a rhetorical flourish, with a final chiasmus: "The question is not how people become real Americans, but how America has become its people."

Made several years before September 11, 2001, *My America* raises issues that remain salient today. Questions of who can "claim" America and who must be excluded from the national body politic due to religion, race, national origin, or ideology continue to vex the popular consciousness. *My America* resonates with the current political climate in which visions of multiculturalism must vie with the excesses of Christian fundamentalism, the Patriot Act, and a xenophobic war mentality brought on by full-scale US incursions into Afghanistan and Iraq. The contradictions around which Tajima-Peña structures her film remain raw, and the humor and transcendence that honking for the love of Buddha imply remain elusive. *My America* takes the high road, traveling through parts of the national landscape and cityscape outside the understanding of the mainstream population, and, even if the search only poses more questions, the journey still needs to be taken.

Cartography and Chronology

My America maps out Asian America in specific ways. As a toy vehicle moves symbolically around a map of the United States, Tajima-Peña bases her real-life travels on patterns of migration that follow racial hierarchies and the vicissitudes of history. Her 2001 essay, "No Mo Po Mo and Other Tales of the Road," provides more information on the way in which *My America* fits within her career as a filmmaker and within her vision of race relations in America. Basing her remarks on extensive research as well as the American life recorded by her camera, she notes: "racial minorities existed in 'colonies' inside the US national borders in conditions much like those of the traditional colonies of imperial powers such as England and France" (247).[6] Throughout the film, she keeps coming back to these "colonies." The Chinese in San Francisco and New York City, the Japanese in California, Chicago, and the interior West of the Internment Camps, the Hmong in Duluth, the Vietnamese in Florida, the Koreans in Seattle and California, and the Filipinos in New Orleans, all have their own enclaves within the American landscape. In fact, these internal colonies are intimately connected to the patterns of colonization of the New World by Europeans. Tajima-Peña picks places connected to Asian American history, and both time and place structure the film around the questions she poses.

In one instance, she travels to New Orleans to highlight the Filipino community living there. The settlement of Filipinos in New Orleans is a direct result of the Spanish galleon trade circumnavigating the globe from Manila to Acapulco, the Caribbean, and the Gulf of Mexico. In 1763 a group of Filipinos jumped ship in New Orleans to escape the Spanish and established the first Asian settlement in what would eventually become the United States.[7] The Burtanog sisters interviewed in the film are, for example, part of the eighth generation of the Filipino community in New Orleans. The China Clipper trade, booming after the British won the Opium Wars, brought Chinese merchants, as well as their merchandise, to ports like New York, and the Gold Rush lured the Chinese to California as miners and, later, laborers on the Union Pacific railroad. Victor Wong, son of the "MSG king" of San Francisco's Chinatown, and Chung Y. Choi, the "fortune cookie king" of New York's Chinatown, represent this bi-coastal mercantile tradition.

However, in spite of their important role in building the American economy, historically the Chinese were constantly under siege from exclusionary laws that severely restricted immigration and imposed on them exorbitant taxes throughout the late nineteenth century, and well into the twentieth. In this context, the 1906 San Francisco earthquake was a boon to the Chinese who benefited from the destruction of immigration records. In the film, Tajima-Peña links this natural disaster to the year her grandfather came to America via San Francisco, was told to "get out of town" by white bigots, and, as a result, ended up avoiding the destruction of the earthquake.

The bombing of Pearl Harbor on December 7, 1941, looms large insofar as it set off a chain of events that had a dramatic impact on the Asian American community. In 1942, President Franklin Delano Roosevelt signed Executive Order 9066, which led to the internment of Japanese Americans. Strikingly, the 442nd Japanese American regiment gained fame during the Second World War for their heroism on the battlefields of Europe.[8] Activists Yuri and Bill Kochiyama—who feature in *My America*—actually met during the war when Bill was on leave and allowed to visit one of the Internment camps. Given that the Japanese who had settled on the West Coast lost everything (homes, businesses, jobs, etc.) because of the Internment, many subsequently relocated to cities like Chicago, even before the war had ended. Since Executive Order 9066 was enforced only selectively (mostly along regional lines), the Japanese living east of the Mississippi River were not interned en masse, making places like Chicago attractive for Japanese Americans. In fact, in 1946 the Japanese American Service Committee (formerly the Resettlers Committee) was formed in Chicago to help with resettlement of Japanese Americans from the concentration camps.[9]

Spanning the decades from the 1940s to the 1990s, interned Japanese Americans and their children continued to agitate for redress. Gradually, grudgingly, it came. In 1976, President Gerald Ford rescinded Executive Order 9066, hearings followed in 1981, an official apology in 1987, and, finally, reparation payments in 1989. From Yuri Kochiyama—who lived in Harlem, supported Malcolm X, and pushed for justice for interned Japanese Americans— to Korean American Alyssa Kang and her involvement with Asian American causes as a student at UCLA in the 1990s (to say nothing about Tajima-Peña's own activism), *My America* highlights Asian American struggles against racism and for civil rights from the 1940s to the present.

Calls for equal rights and civil liberties increased after the war, as blacks and other minorities agitated for social justice. Eventually President Lyndon Johnson signed the Civil Rights Act in 1964, the Voting Rights Act in 1965, and the Immigration and Nationality Act in 1965, which opened the door to increased immigration from Asia. However, the Johnson administration also put the United States on another path with the escalation of the American war in Vietnam after the Gulf of Tonkin incident in 1964. Agitation for civil rights and against the war in Vietnam radicalized a generation of Asian Americans, Renee Tajima-Peña among them. After the fall (or, liberation) of Saigon in 1975, a number of refugees from Vietnam, Laos, and Cambodia left Southeast Asia, many relocating to the United States. Thus in the film, Pan Ku Yang and Tom Vu represent the extremes experienced by the "boat people" in America: from the working poor of the beleaguered northern Midwest to the nouveau riche of the booming "sunshine" states of the southeast coast.

Made after the 1992 uprising in Los Angeles—precipitated by the acquittal of the police who a year earlier beat African American Rodney King (and were caught on videotape)—*My America* looks at the younger generation of Asian

Americans, like the Korean merchants in Los Angeles, still positioned between the black and white cultures.[10] The Korean American rappers, the "Seoul Brothers," of Seattle are juxtaposed with Asian American debutantes in Anaheim, California, who cannot bring their Caucasian boyfriends to the ball. Within her generation, Alyssa Kang strikes a balance between the extremes—the Seoul Brothers' anger and the debs' complacency—so that, in the end, *My America* points with hope toward the future.

The Road Movie

My America fits within the tradition of the American "road movie."[11] The birth of cinema coincided with the advent of the motor vehicle, and the two developed side by side throughout the twentieth century. As highways spread across the United States, especially during the Eisenhower era, and as car culture began to dominate the popular imagination, the road movie sprang up to take advantage of the "new frontier" of the open road. The road, after all, implies a journey, and this brings the road movie in line with the world's greatest literary classics dealing with life as a journey (the *Book of Exodus* from the *Bible*, the *Odyssey*, *Pilgrim's Progress*, and others). The journey can involve escape from the constraints of home, self-discovery within constantly changing, unfamiliar environments, or simply rootless wandering. The characteristically episodic plots of road movies and the loose structure of documentary road films encourage dramatic changes in mood, brief encounters, and apparently aimless drifting. Typically, the journey ends in death, a settled life, or another trip, with the city either a pit stop or else a final destination within the conventions of the genre.

Often the very act of going on the road implies a critique of society, and the road movie is indeed a good vehicle to delve into the causes for America's social ills. The traveler hits the road for a reason, escaping from the strictures of a settled life, looking for freedom, or trying to determine the meaning of the "real" America. In this search for America, key contradictions within the fabric of society come into play, including tensions between individualism and community spirit, between work and leisure, between wilderness and civilization, between rural and urban life, between putting down roots and nomadic movement, between mainstream culture and countercultures, and so on. The road can become a border as well, dividing up the land and positioning people on the other side of the fence or the wrong side of the tracks. Almost by definition, the road involves an encounter with the "other" within the American landscape, making ethnic, racial, and regional differences salient.

My America, like many road movies, involves a trip from coast to coast and a search for a "real" American identity. The protagonist—in this case the filmmaker Renee Tajima-Peña herself—becomes the constant within the changing landscape.

She contrasts her own experiences with those of each person she encounters along the way, and the depth of the country's history and the breadth of the country's geography define her trip. She notes that many Asian Americans have been compelled to take a different road, and she contrasts her trip with her grandfather's forced eviction from his point of disembarkation in San Francisco in 1906. Her grandfather was forced to run; the granddaughter has a choice and can drive instead.

The road movie can take many forms, and *My America* situates itself within the documentary mode (e.g., *Sherman's March*, 1986), the journalistic tradition (e.g., broadcast-news features like "On the Road with Charles Kerault"), and the amorphous film genre of autobiography/family portrait/diary (e.g., *Letters to Ali*, 2004). The nonfiction film goes on the road to make a discovery about the self in relation to others, and to reveal what may be hidden from those who stay put. In fact, the road movie can blur fact and fiction as much as blur the distinctions among various cinematic genres.

At least since the publication of Jack Kerouac's classic book, *On the Road* (1957), road films have held a conversation with a body of "on the road" literature that took the genre in an even more critical direction. Emerging from the Beat subculture, Kerouac's singular journey became a communal rite of passage as the inward spiritual journey evolved in tandem with the physical road trip. In *My America* Tajima-Peña directly references Kerouac through her portrait of Victor Wong, a member of Kerouac's inner circle. However, in place of Kerouac's male-centered journey she situates her own trip in the context of an Asian American woman's search for an America that eluded Kerouac. More mature, Tajima-Peña's road trip functions less as a rite of passage than as a rediscovery of her own past, the history of Asians in America, and the circumstances that unite and divide the country.

In the film Tajima-Peña speaks about her memories of family road trips in their Ford Fairlane, the iconic family car produced between 1955 and 1969. Part of the American road culture, the family road trip has become a staple of the national experience. In addition to images of the highway, however, *My America* provides a home-movie montage of the young Renee with national monuments such as the Statue of Liberty and Mount Rushmore, as well as with popular icons of Americana, such as amusement park trains and beauty pageant winners on parade floats. However, the little Asian girl's face does not blend in easily with the landscape, and it is at that point that Tajima-Peña notes that the family could cross five states and not see another Asian face.

Several road trips structure *My America*: from Tajima-Peña's childhood summer vacations on the road to the Beat generation's journey across America to the adult filmmaker's trip in search of Asian America. The road also provides a metaphor for her vision of America as a land of movement, change, and possibility. The road may come to a dead-end, but another route always seems to open up, allowing one to continue the journey. Despite the tragedies she encounters on the road—from the legacy of the Internment, to the murder of Civil Rights activists in Mississippi, to the death of her own brother—her vision remains stubbornly optimistic. In fact, the then recently married filmmaker expresses her hope to take her children with her on the road one day.

The City Film

The freedom to go on a road trip presupposes a certain class position—the money to buy and maintain a car and the leisure time/disposable income to be able to go on an extended holiday. Others on the road—hitchhikers, vagrants, outlaws, bikers—may be there for very different reasons. In contrast to the road, the city represents a very different sort of movement, connected to a bounded geographical space. Of course, American cinema has as intimate a connection with the city as it does with the road.[12]

The "city film" documents urban life almost like a living organism with its own diurnal rhythms of waking up, preparing for the activities of the day, and going through daily routines. Streets and subways form its arteries, while people circulate throughout it day and night. Many of these films are nothing short of "city symphonies" that celebrate the almost musical rhythms of urban life. The history of the city and portraits of its people, their neighborhoods, and civic institutions form, in fact, the bedrock of the genre. German films such as *Berlin: Symphony of a Great City* (1927) and the Soviet-made *Man with a Movie Camera* (1929) influenced films made in America, including Marie Menken's *Go! Go! Go!* (1964) and Bruce Baillie's *Castro Street* (1966).

Although many city films are celebratory, paying homage to urban life as an emblem of enlightened modernity, others emphasize the "evil" city as a place of despair, violence, desperation, and poverty. Within the documentary tradition, films of that nature highlight social problems such as prostitution, drug trafficking, illegal gambling, juvenile delinquency, and other types of urban crime. Shading off into cinematic fiction, city films primarily overlap with the gangster genre, the mystery, *film noir* and the *policier*. The cityscape often structures the film, and key buildings or transportation systems orient the viewer, as in Akira Kurosawa's adaptation of *King's Ransom*—a New York police procedural from America's acclaimed chronicler of urban life, Ed McBain—into the street jungle of Tokyo (*High and Low*, 1963). But even though horror and supernatural evils may haunt the city, it also serves as the site of urban melodrama, focusing on individuals, couples or families confronting the challenges of city life.

On a lighter note, the city has been the backdrop for scores of musicals, with Hollywood providing the stage in unforgettable blockbusters like *Singin' in the Rain* (1952), New York in another Gene Kelly song-and-dance number, *On the Town* (1949), or even New York's Broadway providing the setting in films like *The Broadway Melody* (1929). In fact, the connection between the urban environment and cinema is in some cases so profound that specific cities have become inextricably linked with movie genres. Prominent among them are Chicago and the gangster film, New York City and the Broadway musical, New Orleans and the "voodoo" horror film, Las Vegas or Miami and the "vice" film, San Francisco and the Western, Detroit and the working-class melodrama, Hollywood and the backstage drama, or Los Angeles and the Chandleresque *noir*. City names figure prominently in film titles to evoke a mood or even a certain type of story. From a multitude of examples, one can mention here *New York, New York* (1977), *Manhattan* (1979), *Maid in Manhattan* (2002), *Gangs of New York* (2002), *Chicago* (2002), *Leaving Las Vegas* (1995), *Fear and Loathing in Las Vegas* (1998), *To Live and Die in LA* (1985), *LA Confidential* (1997), *Old San Francisco* (1927), *Inside Detroit* (1956), and the New Orleans-set *The Big Easy* (1987).

Certainly, *My America* has more in common with the road movie than the city film. In a departure from the latter, for example, it does not concentrate on providing a portrait of any particular city and its inhabitants. This is not to deny, however, that when *My America* stops in the city, it takes on some of the characteristics of the city film. The metropolitan agglomerations she visits, from New York, Chicago, New Orleans, San Francisco, Duluth, Seattle, to Los Angeles, necessarily shape their inhabitants, and Tajima-Peña carefully places each person she interviews within a specific urban and ethnic context. As they unfold before your eyes, the streets of New York contrast sharply with New Orleans, and the social environment of Seattle bears little resemblance to Duluth.

In fact, *My America* uses music and carefully chosen establishing shots to place the American city in the context of mass media clichés, and contrast those culturally dominant images with the way in which Asian Americans live next to (or even in) familiar urban landmarks. Thus the filmmaker as a child, standing next to New York's Statue of Liberty, demands recognition for the urban landscape of America in an immigrant context. The manufacture of fortune cookies takes on the rhythm of New York street life. The New Orleans graveyard becomes a place to discuss the color line and where Asians can be buried. Chicago's Wrigley Field no longer overshadows the city's Japanese American population. The lives of Indochinese refugees become part of the cityscape of Duluth in the frozen Midwest. Los Angeles acknowledges its place on the Pacific Rim and serves as the setting for anti-racist demonstrations in support of the rights of Asians in America. Seattle mixes rap and Asian karaoke. And here old San Francisco offers an alternative view of Chinatown as a site of generational conflict, maturation and promise, so at odds with Hollywood's cooked up (and still lingering) imagery of a den of iniquity and "yellow peril" contagion.

Linking them even as it threads through them, the road allows these contrasting cities to co-exist on the same map, and *My America* positions them dialectically so that conflicting views of Asian America can be juxtaposed and compared. Thus the pace of the city—revolving around interviews, neighborhood tours, and domestic spaces—punctuates the progress of the film. Clearly, if the road has a different meaning for Asians in America, then the city does as well. Tellingly, the confines of Chinatown or subsidized housing for Southeast Asian exiles can exist in close proximity to the possibilities latent in Wall Street or the financial district of San Francisco. Recording and juxtaposing these images, *My America* frames its portraits of Asians within the familiar, yet estranged, American cityscape.

The Personal Journey

My America … or, Honk if You Love Buddha is very much a personal journey. Working within a self-reflexive tradition, the process of making the film mirrors the road trip itself, while the film becomes a portrait of the director/protagonist. At various points, Tajima-Peña reflects on her life and family history to compare her journey and her experiences with those of the Asian Americans she encounters on her travels. In addition to the road trip she makes in the film, Tajima-Peña sees her very life as a journey beginning with her birth in Chicago. Situated in the country's Midwest, Chicago and the state of Illinois become the emblems of middle-America in the film. The small Japanese neighborhood around Wrigley Field, the home turf of one of Chicago's two baseball teams, is home to the brownstone in which she spent her early childhood. She shows the sports field, named after the chewing gum company, accompanied by black blues music on the soundtrack, positioning the Japanese community between middle-American whiteness and Chicago blues.

Her childhood is presented, in fact, in terms of contradictions. Having been raised not to be "too Japanese" and to blend in, she includes images of herself dressed in an Easter bunny suit, a hula skirt, shorts, and posed against a Christmas tree. Referring to the popular 1952–66 television show, she describes her parents as "the Japanese version of Ozzie and Harriet"—ironically, an all-white and all-American family. Yet she also underlines how the entire family dropped everything when any Asian face appeared on television, since the opportunities to see Asians in a public setting were so few and far between. All too frequently, these images were limited to "yellow face" Caucasian actors impersonating the Japanese enemy in the wake of the Second World War, bringing the fact that the Internment had displaced the Tajima family to the surface.

Over photos of her mother's family in the camps and her father in military uniform, Tajima-Peña explains the family's Second World War experience. Her maternal grandfather, for example, looked at camp life as a "big vacation" because he no longer had to work in three jobs, while for her father it meant not seeing military action because of an outbreak of chickenpox just before peace was declared. However, as she revealed later on in an online interview for *Mozaik*, the Internment indelibly marked her and shaped her family history. "The camp experience has always been ingrained in our family lexicon. To this day, whenever

I meet another Japanese American, I ask by way of introduction, 'What camp was your family in?' It is a way of breaking the ice and establishing connections. In my lifetime, I have rarely met another Japanese American with whom I did not have some link, via the camps, family, friends of friends, or our family homestead in Japan."

In 1966, the Tajima family moved to California where, growing up in the 1960s, Renee describes moving from Ozzie-and-Harriet to a hippie phase, a disco phase, and a "wannabe home girl" phase with a puffy Afro hairstyle to match. It was during that time that she became politically active. Using images from the classic documentary, *Fall of the I-Hotel* (Curtis Choy, 1983), she recounts her involvement with protests over the 1977 destruction of the I-Hotel in San Francisco, which housed many Asian American poor. She contrasts the feeling of being for the first time comfortable in her own skin with the uncritical mass mentality that marked the excesses of the counterculture. As "The East Is Red" plays on the soundtrack, cows march toward the camera, chewing their cud, perhaps echoing the marching sheep from the opening of Chaplin's *Modern Times*.

Moving beyond Mao and the youth movement, Tajima-Peña shows nonetheless how activism forged a bond between young Asian Americans and her parents' generation. She observed in the same 2000 interview: "All of my second generation relations—including my parents, aunts and uncles—participated in some way, with a defiance I had never seen before. Through the testimony delivered to the Commission on Wartime Relocation and Internment Camps, we, the next generation, came to appreciate the context of the times, and the depth of the personal nightmare our parents faced" (*Mozaik*). In fact, Tajima-Peña's portrait of her parents changes from TV's Ozzie and Harriet to a gracefully aging couple taking up ballroom dancing, the father growing a stylish beard, as she proudly recounts their court testimony regarding the Internment. The filmmaker's personal journey comes full circle with her own marriage, and the generational differences that underpin the film find a seeming resolution as family life continues.

Both the city film and the road movie feature characters who journey to discover their place, whether within the urban milieu (e.g., the gangster's rise and fall) or within the American landscape (e.g., the road trip as self-discovery). As the protagonist's story unfolds, encounters with characters representing important places, issues, and concerns become central to the pilgrim's physical as well as personal progress. On the road, the characters are the milestones marking the trip; in the city, they represent different strata of urban life even as they are the benchmarks for the transformation in the one who undertakes the journey. True to form, *My America* unfolds as a series of portraits which, as they intersect with the filmmaker's story, become focal points of comparison and contrast with her experience. It is for no other reason that Tajima-Peña selects a range of people from different ethnic groups, experiences of immigration, ages and economic circumstances, and different regions of the country. Part of what she wants to bridge in the film is, in her own words, the "gulf between my own narrow Asian American experience and that of the new Asian immigrants and refugees" (252).

Portraits in Motion

Victor Wong

Actor, photographer and activist, Victor Wong plays a special role in *My America*, beginning with the fact that he has quite a lot in common with Tajima-Peña (he is the "same age as my dad but has the same questions I have"). More importantly, he represents the uncertainty of identity and the slippery nature of the filmmaker's journey, insofar as her encounter with Wong begins with a mistake. Inspired by Wayne Wang's pioneering independent production *Chan Is Missing* (1982), she sets out to interview the actor whom she remembers as the cabbie who scours Chinatown in search of the elusive Chan.[13] However, as she soon discovers, the taxi driver was played by Wood Moy, and Victor Wong was never in the film at all. Contrasting images of Moy and Wong at the wheel, she reflects quizzically: "Maybe we do all look alike?" Perhaps, like the very protagonist of *Chan Is Missing*, Tajima-Peña sets out on a search for a person or an identity that cannot be found. The prospect of a failed search for something that does not exist haunts *My America*.

Son of a leader of Chinatown who made his fortune in MSG, Victor Wong acts as tour guide to San Francisco's Sacramento Street, also known as Tang Ren Jie—the "street of the Tang people," in a reference to the golden era of China's Tang Dynasty (618–907 A.D.). Wong feels confined by the borders of Chinatown and his father's expectations for him, and he has no qualms in describing himself as "the Wong that went wrong." Looking to rebel, he even became a "Jesus freak" preaching on street corners. Given the proximity of Beat institutions, such as City Lights bookstore to San Francisco's Chinatown, he became a fixture in Beat circles, honored with a mention in Jack Kerouac's *Big Sur* (1962).

Associating Chinese women with traditional marriages and his own unhappy family life, Wong married an African American theater director in 1964. Olive Wong, also interviewed in the film, tells the story of their seven year-long marriage that went against the wishes of both sets of parents. Unfortunately, she recounts, her husband treated his wife and children the same way that his father had treated his family. Laments Victor: "We thought there would be a new world. America just wasn't ready." Victor Wong went on to marry and divorce several other times, and *My America* shows him at a family reunion with his children and grandchildren (sadly, his son Lyon, to whom he was particularly close, was killed by a street gang). Tajima-Peña contrasts Wong's complex family with his performance in Wayne Wang's film *Eat a Bowl of Tea* (1989), based on the 1961 novel by Louis Chu in which the "bachelor society" of Chinatown is robbed of women and family life by American exclusionary laws.[14] Trying to create family within a Chinese American community reeling from the history of racist policies proves challenging for Wong in fact and in fiction.

In another link with Tajima-Peña, Wong also spent time in Chicago, as an actor in comedy theater Second City. He recounted to the camera the difficulty he had as an Asian American trying to find a niche within the theater company. Returning to San Francisco to work as a photojournalist, he became fascinated by the faces he encountered in Chinatown. Framing his own face with his hands, he spoke of the tendency in America to conflate all Asian ethnicities into a single "enemy" category, from the Japanese of the Second World War to the Koreans, Chinese, and Vietnamese of the Cold War. He proclaimed: "As an Asian American, I had to write my own manual as to how to live in this country." Although Tajima-Peña looks up to Wong (who passed away in 2001) as "Buddha, Obi-Wan Kenobi, and Kerouac all rolled into one," he continues to pose as many questions as he answers about navigating America with an Asian face.

Chung Y. Choi

Wong, as a romantic ex-Beat, artist, actor and dreamer, stands in marked contrast to another denizen of Chinatown, Chung Y. Choi. Choi makes his home on the opposite coast, in New York, and although both are Chinese Americans, Wong and Choi could not be further apart. Punk music, police cars, accidents, and arguments brand New York City as a different species from the staid San Francisco Chinatown. Tajima-Peña follows Choi as he makes his rounds in his peripatetic search for money. Choi has cornered the market on fortune cookies, runs a fish business, teaches Tae Kwon Do in the Bronx, sells promotional calendars, and works security for lion dancers during Chinese New Year. Tajima-Peña calls him "Horatio Alger on amphetamines," and he has clearly much more in common with Victor Wong's father than with either Wong or Tajima-Peña. Still a man of contradictions, Choi claims to use the girlie calendars in his office to find phone numbers quickly, while he burns incense to Guan Gong—the god of war and enterprise—for a break.

Burtanog Sisters

Moving dialectically, *My America* goes from the North to the South, from New York to New Orleans, from the new immigrant to eighth generation residents. It goes from a man who still very much identifies with his Chinese ethnicity to the Burtanog sisters who see themselves as Americans and Southerners, and only marginally as Filipina or Asian. "The Philippines is not your country," serves as their family mantra. However, the Burtanog sisters enjoyed the privilege of being "honorary whites" in the American South, precisely because the Philippines was a colony of Spain when their ancestors arrived, and its inhabitants were considered Spanish and white. Throughout the Southern history of slavery and segregation, Filipinos could live with, go to school with, marry, and be buried alongside whites—as well as become queens of Mardi Gras. Significantly, those in the Philippine community who intermarried with blacks were shunned for generations, and the color line demarcated the boundaries of their lives.[15]

Yuri and Bill Kochiyama

Yuri and Bill Kochiyama provide counterpoint to the Burtanog sisters. Rather than shunning the African American community, the Kochiyama family embraced it—settling in Harlem, becoming very active in the Civil Rights movement, supporting Malcolm X, etc.[16] Tajima-Peña meets up with them on the road in Mississippi on a visit to Rosedale, where their son Billy (who died in 1975) had been a "freedom rider" agitating for desegregation of the South by crossing the color line on public buses in the 1960s. *My America* introduces Yuri Kochiyama with a camera covering her face, placing her visually with photographer Victor Wong and filmmaker Tajima-Peña as observer/activists documenting the Asian American experience on celluloid.

After visiting the Davis family that had hosted their son, Yuri and Bill go to the grave of James Earl Chaney who had also been killed (with Michael Schwerner and Andrew Goodman) while fighting in support of the Civil Rights movement in 1964. The trip to the South also allows the couple to revisit the places they associate with the Second World War. The Japanese American experience of the Internment parallels life for blacks in the segregated South, and the movement for reparations for camp survivors parallels the Civil Rights movement. The Kochiyama family places Asian Americans and African Americans in the same fight for justice and racial equality in America. Part of the 442nd regiment, Bill Kochiyama had been stationed at Camp Shelby, Mississippi, during the war. On leave, he was given a pass to go to Jerome, Arkansas, where he met Yuri who was interned there. In the film the couple visit the site of the Jerome Internment camp and find only a single tower standing. A local farmer informs them that the camp was bulldozed under the field, adding that the interned Japanese were "good people" who did not deserve to be imprisoned. Moved, Yuri documents the encounter with a photograph as Tajima-Peña captures it on film.[17]

Because the all-Japanese American 442nd saw so much action, Bill Kochiyama did not want to marry Yuri until the end of the war. They had both been moved by the number of young widows in the war's wake, so they married after Bill's discharge and settled in New York's Harlem. The entire family participated actively in the Civil Rights movement; in fact, Yuri Kochiyama was on stage with Malcolm

X when he was assassinated in 1965. Both continued to be active in the anti-war movement as well as in the movement for reparations for Internment survivors. (Bill Kochiyama passed away in 1993 before the completion of *My America*; Yuri later moved to be with her surviving family in California.)

Tom Vu and Pan Ku Yang

From looking at the lives the Kochiyamas, who agitated against the war in Vietnam, *My America* moves to the life stories of Tom Vu and Pan Ku Yang, who settled in America because of their support for the losing side in the war. Tom Vu left Vietnam in 1975 after the country was reunified under the Communist government. As Tajima-Peña remarks in voice-over, she had "red" visions of the East under Mao, while "Tom Vu was in refugee camps dreaming that the West was green—greenbacks green." Now a millionaire, Tom Vu is shown in a Rolls Royce as he explains his get-rich-quick scheme through real estate speculation. His motivational videos feature statuesque Caucasian models listening carefully to his methods. However, as the poor rural Florida blacks are contrasted with Vu's opulent lifestyle, Tajima-Peña notes that Vu is under investigation by the Florida State Attorney's Office.

Moving from Florida to Minnesota, *My America* looks to another American millionaire as a bridge between Tom Vu and Pan Ku Yang. Tajima-Peña goes in search of Jeno Paulucci, the Italian American who became the frozen Chinese egg-roll king. Instead, she finds refugee garment workers from Laos.[18] Unlike Vu, these displaced people had difficulties finding green pastures in the United States. From the rural interior highlands of Indochina, these minority Hmong people supported American troops in remote areas. While many urban Vietnamese brought connections, capital and entrepreneurial skills with them, the Hmong from Laos only knew the life of farming and fighting. After the war, they were relocated to less desirable locations in the "rustbelt" of America and to public housing in inner city areas. People like Pan Ku Yang and her husband drifted into industries already on the skids, such as garment manufacturing and canning.

As the children's song "This Is the United States of America" plays on the soundtrack, *My America* portrays the gulf between Pan Ku Yang and her husband and their children. The children play in the snow, buy penny candy, play video games and watch television. Their staples are the *Tom and Jerry* cartoons, while their unemployed father watches a video featuring Laotian pop stars. In Pan Ku Yang's suitcase is her traditional dress as well as a quilt she embroidered to commemorate her escape from the communist regime in Laos—and the death of four children there. In the United States, in addition to living in public housing and struggling to keep a low-paying job, Pan Ku Yang also faces racism. Like Tajima-Peña's grandfather in 1906, she is taunted by racist remarks and told to get out of town. After her moving story of survival, Tajima-Peña chooses not to ask Pan Ku Yang about her feelings regarding Asian American identity. The filmmaker observes: "She knows who she is and where she comes from."

Mike and Raphael Park

Tom Vu and Pan Ku Yang find themselves in America because of the United States' military presence in Asia. For similar reasons, South Korean immigration has been facilitated by America's continuing military and economic ties to that divided nation. Rather than coming as refugees, many Koreans, however, come to America as students, technicians, and entrepreneurs to work in high-tech industries. Many open small businesses in areas often abandoned by whites, for example in inner-city or predominantly African American and Hispanic neighborhoods.

Born in Seoul, South Korea, and raised in Seattle, Mike and Raphael Park strongly identify with African American youth culture and rap music. Billing themselves as the "Seoul Brothers," they rap about living in America as young Asian men. Their admiration for Malcolm X connects them to Yuri and Bill Kochiyama, and like Malcolm and the Panthers they advocate the use of violence to redress racial injustice "by any means necessary." Although the parents disagree with their views, they encourage their sons' musical and creative aspirations. In a pointed contrast to Asian American debutantes' preference for non-Asian boyfriends, the Park brothers rap about Asian masculinity. Upset by Asian women's apparent preference for Caucasian men, the rappers pen the song "Just like Honey" to serve as an enticing advertisement for Asian virility and love as sweet as honey. However, the Park parents remain conservative, and the brothers note that no girl has yet "passed the Mom test." Anti-Asian racism and traditional attitudes toward sexuality conspire to keep the Park brothers single.

Alyssa Kang

Korean-American student activist, Alyssa Kang, serves as a corrective to both the Park brothers' machismo and the Asian American debutantes' aversion to their own community. Raised by her mother after being abandoned by an abusive father, Alyssa Kang has a healthy suspicion of the Asian patriarchy. In fact, this resonates with the director's own family history, since Tajima-Peña's grandmother had been ostracized by the Japanese community because of the circumstances of her birth, leaving Japan at the age of twenty. America opened up the promise of leaving certain aspects of patriarchal tradition behind as part of the immigrant experience. However, Kang still firmly identifies with the community and works as an advocate for Korean immigrant workers. Although the legacy of Japan's colonization of Korea should set them apart, Asian American activism brings Renee Tajima-Peña and Alyssa Kang together as sisters in a common cause.

After a brief stint as a "young Republican," Alyssa Kang quickly turned to more progressive political activities. Studying at UCLA (which, Tajima-Peña notes, has been dubbed "the university of Caucasians lost among Asians"), Kang became an important campus activist, and she was arrested in an anti-Proposition 187 sit-in at Murphy Hall by LAPD officers. Passed by California voters in 1994, Proposition 187 sought to deny public benefits to illegal immigrants. Public outrage from the immigrant community and various progressive civil rights organizations at what was likely an unconstitutional piece of legislation came to a boil. Eventually, when Gray Davis was elected in 1998, the will to enforce the proposition withered. However, many students, like Alyssa Kang, politicized by the struggle against Proposition 187 continue to be active as new versions of old exclusionary laws cling to the American body politic.

The End of the Road

While many tales of the road come to the end of the journey with death, marriage and the settled life, or the beginning of another odyssey, *My America* concludes with all three. Three deaths of young Asian men punctuate the film—the death of Yuri and Bill Kochiyama's son Billy, Victor Wong's son Lyon, and Renee Tajima-Peña's brother Bobby. The passing away of these young men represent the perils of living in urban America, and they symbolize the human potential thwarted before it could take root and blossom. However, *My America* also celebrates the settled life with the Kochiyama's long and happy marriage, Victor Wong's family reunion with his new wife, children, and grandchildren, and the filmmaker's marriage to her Hispanic groom.

Even as the film affirms family life and new beginnings, it concludes with a fresh question and potentially fresh journey by querying not how immigrants assimilate into the American melting pot, but how the United States changes in response to her people. As Tajima-Peña pointed out in her *Mozaik* interview: "In meeting many different Asian Americans in the making of this film, I realized that we would not be distinguished by our level of assimilation (i.e., Americanization) and how people become Americans, but rather how America has become its people." As her film continues to pose questions, the road beckons to a new generation of Asian Americans through Tajima-Peña's hopes for her children. Other filmmakers have also gone on the road to search for the community's history within the American landscape and cityscape. Loni Ding's *Ancestors in America* video series (1998), for example, narrates the saga of Asian immigrants from the seventeenth through the twentieth centuries. Similarly, Canadian filmmaker Richard Fung has gone on the road to look for the history of queer Asians on the railroad in *Dirty Laundry* (1996). For Fung, Ding, and Tajima-Peña, the road does not end in the city, but passes through it, inviting people to celebrate change and embrace a multicultural, multiracial, multiethnic America.

CHAPTER 3

A Is for American, B Is for Bad, C Is for City:

ED McBAIN AND THE ABC OF POLICE AND URBAN PROCEDURALS

Peter Swirski

Born Salvatore Albert Lombino before legally changing his name in 1952, Evan Hunter is a popular writer *par excellence*. Writing as Ed McBain, his bestselling cycle of 87th-Precinct police procedurals won him the loyalty of generations of readers, with sales to prove it: more than 100 million worldwide. Yet even critics of the more apocalyptic persuasion (to use Eco's parlance) would find it hard to dismiss him as a generic crowd pleaser.[1] Over half a century of writing the world's longest running crime-fiction soap, his fifty-six volume opus has drawn praise from just about everyone, including the literary mavens. The *New York Times Book Review* has a hard time deciding whether his prose is dazzling or only formidable, the normally reticent *Guardian* dubs him a virtuoso, and Jeff Zalesky sums up the consensus in *Publishers Weekly*: "McBain is so good he ought to be arrested" (54).

Criminal and forensic investigations are central to every 87th-Precinct novel. This is crime fiction, make no mistake about it. True to form, McBain's heroes are the sparsely drawn cops who process crime scenes as often as they comment on the American way of life. But his principal "character" is as extraordinary as the ending of Hitchcock's *Birds* (for which he wrote the screenplay). It is not a person, even though he personifies "her" in every novel. It is a place, a metaphor, and a state of mind. It is a habitat overrun by human species populating America today. It is, as in the eponymous title of his 1999 bestseller, *The Big Bad City*. While there are sufficient clues to identify its real-life archetype, the author never names the metropolis he describes with so much passion. Instead, he precedes every book with a formal disclaimer: "The city in these pages is imaginary. The people, the places are all fictitious. Only the police routine is based on established investigatory technique."

As a sociological barometer of *urbs Americana*, McBain's fiction may be as good as it gets but, like everything else, all good things must come to an end. The author's death in July 2005 put an effective end to the 87th-Precinct series—that is, unless a lesser talent is hired to take over the reins, something the master vowed never to let happen. With this in mind, he actually intended to tie up all loose ends—perhaps by burying a few cops of his own—in the final instalment of the series, called *Exit*. As it is, the public will have to make do with the posthumously released *Fiddlers*. Be that as it may, McBain's own exit provides an opportune moment for a retrospective on his artistic legacy.

With Hammett's and Cain's hardboiled act swept away by the postwar boom, with Chandler transforming the tough-guy canon in his sentimental *The Long Goodbye* and self-reflexively parodic *Playback*, the 1950s were fertile ground for a new brand of crime story.[2] Mickey Spillane's anti-communist crudities notwithstanding, gone were the days of a solitary sleuth with a Webley .455 for hire. The law-and-order business was now the provenance of a rank professional, a graduate of police academy, a career member of a civic bureaucracy, a specialized cog in a well-greased investigative machine. After the Mafia syndication and the failure to federally regulate the illegal drug industry, crime was too organized to leave it to a bunch of rumpled loners, no matter how lethal their side-of-the mouth drawl.

Enter the police procedural with its stress on the realism of forensic technique, on the nitpicking detail of investigative routine, and the nuance of mundane police work. Today, with former cops like Joseph Wambaugh or former criminal-court reporters like John Katzenbach fusing first-hand experience with artistic élan, dishing out urban realism in quality fiction is almost a given. "Have you ever seen Mike Hammer or Sam Spade spend their days poring over statements like old bloody book-worms?", mutters a jaded Chief Inspector in *The Hatchet Man*, a 1976 procedural by William Marshall. A reply from his equally tired detective sums up a revolution in worldview. "They weren't cops. They were private eyes" (137).

It was the hardboiled masters who took crime out of a British drawing room and dumped it in the middle of the American backstreet. But it was McBain who tossed it in the back of a city cruiser on a jumble of tabloids, junk food litter, crack spoons, economic avarice, me-first mentality, and racial prejudice. One of the first to put the good, bad, and ugly cops in narrative limelight, McBain even rode shotgun with the blues to absorb their workaday MO and that curious babel of bureaucratese, slang, and underworld idiolect that makes up copspeak. Famed for his trademark realism and perfect-pitch ear for dialogue, his prose would even go on to inspire one of the most successful—because the most realistically low-key—TV police shows, *Hill Street Blues*.

Whence the attraction to, if not exactly affection for, the City? The reasons are not hard to deduce. With New York as the representative cityscape, the 87th Precinct is an anatomy of the environmental niche overrun by more than 80 percent of all North Americans. Inhabited by millions, preyed upon by thousands, immortalized in prose from Thomas Wolfe and Lawrence Sanders to Tom Wolfe and Colin Harrison, McBain's City is a creature of beauty frequently described in lyrical terms that echo the opening sequence of Woody Allen's *Manhattan*. Even so, the gritty canons of the police procedural—the genre he established almost single-handedly in 1956 with *Cop Hater*—always lead back to the city morgue and to the rotting core of today's Headline News America.

McBain is a master of dialogue of people in all walks of life and ethnic backgrounds. He is a master of description of their lives, rich and affluent, materially and culturally destitute, or driven and riven by crime. And behind them there are always busy city streets, where the narrator's eye glides past little Italian bakeries and coffee shops humming with chitchat, past old theatres and new modelling agencies, through slums and ghettos to smoke-filled, cramped, stinky of coffee and urine rooms of the Precinct station house. The 87th's procedurals are a daily docket of the City's celebrity high-fliers and criminal lowlifes, blowing each other kisses while whisked away on the gravy train or blowing each other away with shotguns.

This love-and-hate, night-and-day, Jekyll-and-Hyde personification of the urban sprawl is quintessential McBain. A genre writer *par excellence*, he has the literary flair and sociological vision to belie cultural conservatives for whom popular fiction belongs, in Harold Bloom's phrase, on the compost heap of popular culture. Charting the rugged and drugged myths of the twentieth-century metropolitan frontier, his police procedurals cross over into the domain of *urban* procedurals to stand next to *The Quaker City*, *The Jungle*, *An American Dream* and *The Bonfire of the Vanities*.

Among unputdownable thrills, chills and kills, McBain records the daily detritus of life in an overpopulated shark tank. Book after book, he reproduces topographical sketches, traffic signs, street signs, licence plates, ferry schedules, airline schedules, handwritten notes, business cards, personal letters, address-book pages, passbook entries, phone-book listings, prescription drug labels, utility bills, telephone bills, credit card bills, personal cheques, letters from the editor, photographs, modelling portfolios, advertising photos, media headlines, tabloid clippings, stage diagrams, theatre programs, and even architectural blueprints. The series is an equal treat for the aficionado of literate crime and a tenured sociologist.

Although the 87th is set elliptically in New York, mismanagement and vice, political bigotry and ethnic strife, loneliness and violence are facts of life in any metropolis. Designed to convey even in typography the feel of the municipal machine, the impact of McBain's documentary aesthetics is hardly confined to America. Fans of Britain's Inspector Morse—between 1987 and 2000 also an acclaimed TV series—will not miss how Colin Dexter packs his cycle with the same litter of daily life that has come to define the 87th Precinct.[3] Handwritten notes, news columns, obituaries, last will, poster, hotel receipt, *Police Gazette* puzzle, diploma, drawings, Medical Examiner's forensic report, letter franking chops, wall plaque, even a vehicle licence plate—all appear in just one book, the last one in the series: *The Remorseful Day*. Just as in McBain, the Morse procedurals are a *vade mecum* to London Town's posh parklands, tawdry tenements, and everything in between. And, just as in McBain, they use the typographic inserts as a legend to the topographical map of the city that coalesces before the reader's eyes.

Visitors to the Hong Kong of William Marshall's Yellowthread Street cycle find themselves in equally familiar territory. *The Hatchet Man*, to take one example, reproduces a postmortem report, ballistics report, lab report, eyewitness statement, police bulletin, Public Relations Department press release, consular report, transcript of interview with a victim, and even the lid of an ammunition box. No less a pointer to McBain is the short disclaimer that precedes every instalment of Detective Chief Inspector Harry Feiffer & Co. "The Hong Bay district of Hong Kong is fictitious, as are the people who, for one reason or another, inhabit it." Nor will the fans of the Swedish masters, Maj Sjöwall and Per Wahlöo—authors of Martin Beck procedurals including the bestselling *The Laughing Policeman* (1969)—miss their tribute to the American author. McBain's Tweedledum-and-Tweedledee homicide dicks, Monroe and Monoghan, are reincarnated as the equally dimwit and inseparable Stockholm patrolmen Kvant and Kristiansson, both pairs priceless in their comic-relief cameos.

The connection with Sjöwall and Wahlöo is far from coincidental. In keeping with McBain's documentary aesthetics, the Swedish authors harnessed their procedurals to much more than the cat-and-mouse game of cops and robbers or narcs and dealers. As revealed in their artistic manifesto, in the Martin Beck decalogue they programmatically set out to "use the crime novel as a scalpel cutting open the belly of the ideological pauperized and morally debatable so-called welfare state of the bourgeois type."[4] Declarations of this nature once again belie the generic perception of detective fiction as subliterature. Do they legitimate, however, the procedural as a sociological and ideological barometer of *Urbs Americana?* For an answer I turn to Ed McBain who, with each re-enactment of *Murder, He Wrote*, delivers a ten-bucks-a-pop lesson in Big Bad City civics.

"I have the most important and corrupt department in New York on my hands"

– Theodore Roosevelt, Police Commissioner (1895)

Detective fiction has come a long way since 1905 when it first got its own heading in *The Reader's Guide to Periodical Literature*. Dominant in terms of sales—detective stories and mysteries generate between them more than a quarter of *all* fiction sold in America—its career is equally impressive in terms of title selection. With only eleven titles listed in the United States in 1952, at subsequent ten-year intervals *Bowker's Global Books in Print* puts the tally at 42, 164, 838, 1,971, and no less than 3,207 titles in the year 2002.[5] Needless to say, even these impressive figures are demonstrably low. For example, even though it is restricted only to what's been produced since the Second World War, Mike Ashley's *Mammoth Encyclopedia of Modern Crime Fiction* (2002) weighs in at eight hundred pages. Allen Hubin's *Crime Fiction II: Comprehensive Bibliography 1749–1900* itemizes no less than 81,000 book titles, not counting individual short stories in more than 4,500 collections.

Colossal both in absolute and relative terms, these statistics testify to the phenomenal appeal of fictional cops and killers. They also beg the obvious question: Whence the popularity of what is, after all, a singularly dirty and thankless profession? Why heroic cops instead of heroic garbagemen or proctologists? The rise of homegrown crime literature is often traced to generalizations about American history, a heritage of violence, frontier mentality and vigilante justice. While true, their role behind the emergence of the first modern detective story, Poe's *The Murders in the Rue Morgue* (1841), is arbitrary at best. Violence, frontier mindset, and vigilantism have been part of the American way long before Poe, without producing crime literature in the modern sense. The less mythopoeic and more accurate truth is that art was a faithful mirror of reality, and that the rise and the nature of American crime fiction parallelled the rise of modern crime and modern police.

Until the early nineteenth century, the means of upholding law and order in cities remained essentially unchanged from the days of Shakespeare. Court-appointed constables (with powers of arrest and occasional detective duties) oversaw city commerce in daytime, while unpaid civilian watchmen patrolled select parishes or precincts at night. Although the 1731 Montgomerie Charter obliged all male New Yorkers to serve on patrols, the middle class routinely relegated the duty to ill-paid irregulars, even as cities and crime swelled beyond control. Exploding in size, urban centers bred poverty, vice, unpaved streets, and sewage-filled open gutters. Wall Streets, posh residential areas and shopping districts rose alongside industrial parks, tenement slums, and inner-city ghettos for blacks, Italians, Greeks, Poles, Russians, and all others who didn't fit the WASP mould. Its denizens were paying the price of progress from old-time homogenous municipal entities to modern molochs.

In 1800 there were six American settlements with a population above 4,000—then the census cutoff for being classified as a city (it has dropped to 2,500 since). In 1900 there were almost five hundred. Record levels of mainly East and South European immigrants—9 million between 1880 and 1900 alone—staggered onto the shores of Ellis Island. But, unlike their earlier brethren, instead of heeding Horace Greeley and heading out west, most chose to stay put in the Big Bad City. In this they were joined en masse by native refugees from New England whose rural communities almost overnight suffered a catastrophic decline. Even as New England's population rose by 20 percent overall, almost 1,000 out of her 1,500 townships shrank at the same time.[6]

From students robbing graves to supply teaching hospitals with cadavers, to the inundation of waterfront violence and regular Blacks vs Irish riots (following the latter's takeover of the domestic service market), New York was the national pace-setter. But with national unemployment hitting 4 million during the depression in the 1890s, other cities did not fare better. Shuddered Rudyard Kipling after visiting Chicago at the century's turn: "I desire urgently never to see it again. It is inhabited by savages" (207). In the 1820s Thomas Jefferson branded American cities as ulcers on the body politic. Reviving Jefferson's horror of the asphalt jungle, in 1901 columnist Percy Grant charged that "Cities have been called ulcers," proceeding with an anatomy of their "filth, poverty and vice" (555) for the readers of *Everybody's Magazine*. The president of Cornell, Andrew D. White, grimly concurred: "With very few exceptions, the city governments in the United States are the worst in Christendom."[7]

All the same, when Britain established its London Metropolitan police in 1829 (detective division in 1842), the fears that the police would become a standing army or an apparatus of political repression became, if anything, even greater in the US. Combined with hostility to regulation—high among immigrants wary of restrictions routine in the old world—were a suspicion of a British import, an absence of ingrained notions of social decorum, a legacy of vigilante justice, prejudice against standing armies, a large itinerant population, decentralized legislative authority, and not least rife ethnic and racial problems. Little wonder that, when the first departments were created in New York (1845) and Chicago (1854), no heed was paid to the mental or physical alacrity of these as-yet uniformless cops.

Funding was so scarce that in the city of 600,000, only nine men comprised the total of Chicago daytime police (to put this in perspective, today's NYPD of almost 39,000 would field a force of 120). Ironically, patrolmen were not even permitted to carry firearms. Only in the 1880s did Philadelphia and Boston arm their men, and New York a decade later still. Exacerbated by political bosses who ran police departments like private fiefdoms, corruption and mismanagement rotted the system in no time at all. Twenty-two years after the birth of NYPD, the State Legislature fired all of New York's cops, declaring the city "too corrupt to govern itself."[8] It was no different with detective squads, created in Boston (1846), New York (1857), Philadelphia (1859), and Chicago (1861) when beat coppers proved an insufficient deterrent. Underpaid and overworked, investigators proved no more resilient than beat cops to the abiding allure of the easy sleazy.

All this is why around that time the first licensed private eyes appear in America. Most were ex-constables who lost work when municipalities began to set up police departments. The need for law-enforcement was so high that in St. Louis, Baltimore and Philadelphia private detective agencies sprang up even before police departments did. In Chicago, Allan Pinkerton opened shop in 1851, cashing in on the hardships cities faced in dealing with crime owing to the rank unprofessionalism of the regular police. Pinkerton's Agency actually offered to take over municipal policing at two-thirds of the price with a guarantee "that the citizens would actually be protected."[9] Tellingly, the offer was declined. In 1887 George Walling summed up his experience of the Big Bad City in *Recollections of a New York Chief of Police: an official record of thirty-eight years as a patrolman, detective, captain, inspector and chief of the New York Police*. His words were as pithy as they were uncompromising: "... in New York there is less liberty and protection of property than in almost any city of Europe, Russian cities not excepted" (600).

The rising tide of crime and poor policing were acute enough to move parts of society to try to create wholesome citizens by moral reform. Even more typical than the state of Maine which, in a harbinger of the Prohibition, declared itself legally dry in 1846, were the New York Society for the Suppression of Vice and the New York Society for the Prevention of Crime. Both aimed to eradicate crime by bringing the social controls of small-town America to the chaos of the modern metropolis. Among others, the Vice Societies sought to improve mores by suppressing and banning crime fiction, citing examples of youths who allegedly ran afoul of the law after reading story-papers and dime novels. In a campaign to abolish crime by abolishing it from the printed page, they even cornered the Massachusetts legislature into a different kind of prohibition. In a move reprised during the anti-comic book hysteria of the 1950s and the Senate hearings on art content in the 1980s, Massachusetts politicians banned sales to minors of books or magazines containing police reports or accounts of criminal deeds (unwittingly testifying to the popularity of crime fiction).[10]

And all this time, fed by immigration, cities grew. Between 1880 and 1900 alone, New York City expanded from under 2 million to 3.5. Urban planners passed zoning laws which segregated populations from one another. Virtually without police supervision, some 300,000 Italians formed a city within a city ruled by the increasingly organized Cosa Nostra. With homicide rates more than double those in the equally industrial and urban England, violence was spinning out of control. Laying bare the rot in Tammany Hall, the turn-of-century Lexow Investigations named NYPD as one of the chief culprits. Cops were involved in wholesale election fraud in return for sinecures from politicos. Patrolmen and officers routinely bought their promotions and, to recoup on expenses, ran a city-wide extortion racket from brothels, saloons and gambling houses. As before, the corruption was not unique to New York. In Denver the Police and Fire Board openly refused to enforce the law. When the Governor acted to remove them, they refused to be fired, fighting pitched battles with the state militia until President Cleveland sent in federal troops to stop further bloodshed.[11]

Not accidentally, it was around that time that American crime literature began to acquire its distinctive character. Its hard edge and penchant for topical realism was due to the fact that many writers of the era were journalists or editors employed by the "slicks," a new type of general magazine that pushed investigative journalism. Unlike old-style detective yarns, hardboiled crime was contemporary in tone and narrated against the backdrop of current events, drifting towards urban realism and its common ills. Muckraking exposés replaced the timetables needed to crack the alibis of Colonel Mustard and Lady Buxom. Eschewing Victorian diction and decorum, the style became understated, geared towards precision and parsimony of expression. The hero was no longer an armchair ace à la Mycroft Holmes or Hercule Poirot but an active investigator with sleeves rolled up to his arms. The crime was no longer an isolated incident to be investigated at leisure but an open-ended violation in a corrupt social system requiring an urgent and active response.

Even the titles revealed parallels between what muckrakers were up to in the real world and what PIs faced in fiction. Melville D. Post's *The Powers that Prey* was a fitting companion to Arthur B. Reeve's "The Campaign Grafter" and Samuel H. Adams's "The One Best Bet", in which the detective goes after crooked politicians. The greatest difference between these early chronicles of crime and the procedurals of today resides not in their tone and style, but in their lingering optimism. Crime, no matter how rife and ferocious, is not yet seen as a threat to the American way of life. Underneath its temporary and localized aberrations, imply the authors, lies a healthy society. It would take Hammett's dog-eat-dog cynicism, Chandler's melancholy rhapsody to corruption, Wambaugh's tragic comedies, and McBain's urban grit to paint the country in a different light.

All this is to say that domestic crime fiction did not come into its own until it came to terms with American social and urban geography. Instead of a static, homogenous, small-town setting, it had to deal with a sprawling, dark, urban nightmare. Instead of ratiocinating a logical proof of crime, the detectives had to mingle with the underworld in order to unearth information before they could pursue criminals in the hostile city. The history of police and crime in the United States shaped the crime story, in that sense making it the quintessential American genre. Unmasking corruption in high places, tracking vice in the police corps, reporting realistic crime in realistic language, the procedural was a literary convention and a response to the twentieth-century metropolis, exposing the tension between the public and the bureaucracy supposed to protect it. Put simply, American crime writers did not have to invent the genre. They wrote about what they saw around them, cruising—as McBain did—the streets of the naked city.

"High Heels on Wet Pavement"
– Michael Millis (1999)

"Among the mystery writers who first influenced me were Raymond Chandler, and Dashiell Hammett and James M. Cain," admitted McBain in a 2000 interview.[12] He could hardly have selected better models. Hammett, at one point a Pinkerton Op himself, was the first to break new ground by creating an investigator hardened by crime but powerless to stop himself from wanting to do something about it. By hook or by crook, the Continental Op had to rid Poisonville of corrupt politicos, crooked power brokers, less than licit lawyers, gang leaders, and other organized offenders.

McBain's Detective Second Grade, Steve Carella, could be a blood relative of the Op, even though by Carella's time the "lone wolf" methods and lifestyle had gone out of fashion. Where Hammett's shamus was a one-man show, for the boys on the squad their significant other is their partner. Where the tough guys celebrated busting a few downtown skulls with a Scotch in one hand and a fast femme on the other, the bulls shun alcohol when on duty, assiduously Mirandize their suspects, and file reports in tedious triplicate. Where private eyes' private lives were so private they hardly existed at all, many of the 87th Precinct's cops rush home in tatty sedans to their families and wives.

Old habits die hard, though, and in the 2003 introduction to *Killer's Payoff* McBain recalled his first publisher's demands for a more sexy approach to one member of the squad. To his credit, McBain stuck to his guns and resisted the pressure to turn Cotton Hawes "into a goddamn private eye" (xvii). So thorough was the breakaway from the hardboiled template that Carella, the series' leading man, was actually disparaged by the same Pocket Books executive for being "not a hero but a married man" (xiii). Completing McBain's makeover was the debut of less than glamorous law-breakers. The larger-than-life Elihu Willsson and king-size Gutman gave way to career felons, so much so that the first four instalments in the series—*Cop Hater, The Mugger, The Pusher, The Con Man*—were entitled after the variety of criminal a real-life policeman might actually encounter. All this was firmly in keeping with McBain's overarching desire to provide "a realistic look at a squad room of cops who, when put together, would form a conglomerate hero in a mythical city" (xv).

Yet, among these transformations of the hardboiled matrix, none is more striking than the departure of the femme fatale. Hard on the trail of Dinah Brand and Brigid O'Shaughnessy, the genre connoisseur would look in vain in all the obvious places. One could hardly be blamed for concluding that she had vanished for good among red-light show girls, executive escorts, Hollywood madams, and other gold-diggers chasing fortunes during the postwar decades (or doing penance in upstate pens). But like other narrative mainstays from the glory days, in McBain's hands the femme fatale had only undergone a dramatic face-lift. Seductive and ubiquitous, she is as constant a fixture as she was when tough mugs rode into the sunset, gats blazing from getaway flivvers' running boards. Ritzy and glitzy one moment, cheap and downright sleazy the next, she still seduces all while belonging to none. Only now she's no longer a player making her moves in the city. Now she *is* the City.

McBain's naturalism can be as gritty as carpark cement, even as his vignettes of City life pulsate with still-life lyricism reminiscent of Pablo Neruda. This melange of illiterate street argot and prose poetry gives his metropolis her own voice. In most hardboiled novels the mood is invariably in the key of melancholy monotone. In contrast, McBain's narrator jump-cuts through a rainbow of emotions, voices and points of view. But the most significant difference is the narrative function played by the City. In private-eye adventures it is rarely more than an ominous backdrop, or at best a stage on which taciturn players act out their violence, greed, and sex-fuelled fantasies. In contrast, McBain's Gotham is the ultimate femme fatale. Female killers, seductresses, lovers and grifters still strut their stuff, but by far the most bewitching of them is the City, her heart high-rise steel and bullet-proof glass.

From clues strewn over the years a seasoned reader will easily identify this queen of American cities as New York. "The city for which these men worked was divided into five geographical sections. The center of the city, Isola, was an island, hence its name: 'isola' *means* 'island' in Italian. In actual practice, however, the *entire* city was casually referred to as Isola" (*Mischief*, 248). Lest there be any mistake about the Big Bad Apple—and the typography in *Kiss* guarantees there isn't—there is but one megasprawl in New York State to befit being called the M*E*T*R*O*P*O*L*I*S*! The cover of *Cop Hater*, the procedural that started it all, strikingly depicts the mundane detritus of real-life cops: bullet holes, spent cartridges, a tattered police shield, blood spatter, typewritten documents. Completing the transformation from a police to an urban procedural, the cover of *Big Bad City* strikingly shows the quintessential gateway to New York City: The Brooklyn Bridge.

All the same, in the 1999 introduction to the new edition of *Cop Hater*, McBain cautioned readers against transposing Manhattan straight onto Isola. "It is next to impossible to overlay a map of my city on a map of New York," he pointed out, for reasons which turn out to be pragmatic as much as aesthetic.[13] On the one hand, even when assisted by a full-time researcher, he found it too hard to verify every detail of New York City before putting it down on the page. On the other, it was simply too much fun to create a living metropolis parallel to the one around him. Liberated from its real-life twin, "The city, then, became a character."

And what a character she is. Her majesty and radiance are in evidence from the first scene on the first page of the first novella. "From the river bounding the city on the north, you saw only the magnificent skyline. You stared up at it in something like awe, and sometimes you caught your breath because the view was one of majestic splendor…. And at night, coming down the River Highway, you were caught in a dazzling galaxy of brilliant suns, a web of lights strung out from the river and then south to capture the city in a brilliant display of electrical wizardry … The traffic lights blinked their gaudy eyes and along The Stem, the incandescent display tangled in a riot of color and eye-aching splash" (*Cop Hater*, 1–2). *The Mugger* opens with a confession: "The city could be nothing but a woman," and continues in a prose sonnet:

Figure 3.1
The book that started it all:
the first police procedural,
Cop Hater (1956)

Figure 3.2
The urban procedural that
sums up the 87th Precinct,
The Big Bad City (1999)

You know her tossed head in the auburn crowns of moulting autumn foliage, Riverhead, and the park. You know the ripe curve of her breast where the River Dix moulds it with a flashing bolt of blue silk. Her navel winks at you from the harbour in Bethtown, and you have been intimate with the twin loins of Calm's Point and Majesta. She is a woman, and she is your woman, and in the fall she wears a perfume of mingled wood smoke and carbon dioxide, a musky, musty smell bred of her streets and of her machines and of her people.

You have known her fresh from sleep, clean and uncluttered. You have seen her naked streets, have heard the sullen murmur of the wind in the concrete canyons of Isola, have watched her come awake, alive, alive.

You have seen her dressed for work, and you have seen her dressed for play, and you have seen her sleek and smooth as a jungle panther at night, her coat glistening with the pin-point jewels of reflected harbor light. You have known her sultry, and petulant, and loving and hating, and defiant, and meek, and cruel and unjust, and sweet, and poignant. You know all of her moods and all of her ways.

She is big and sprawling and dirty sometimes, and sometimes she shrieks in pain, and sometimes she moans in ecstasy.

But she could be nothing but a woman. (1)

McBain's tableaux of city-as-femme-fatale are as passionate as they are frequent. Peering between the covers of *Give the Boys a Great Big Hand*, you might be forgiven for double-checking whether you opened *The Mugger* again. "The city is a woman, you understand. It could be nothing but a woman … And, like a woman, the city generates love and hate, respect and disesteem, passion and indifference. She is always the same city, always the same woman, but oh the faces she wears, oh the magic guile of this strutting bitch. And if you were born in one of her buildings, and if you know her streets and know her moods, then you love her" (142). Strewn over fifty years and more than fifty books, such urban lyrics punctuate the daily refrain of murder and strife. In the December of *Mischief*, the City turns Cinderella-like into "a dazzling snow princess in silver and white" (295). In the April of *The Heckler* she *is* April, "a delicate thing who walked into the city with the wide-eyed innocence of a maiden, and you wanted to hold her in your arms because she seemed alone and frightened in this geometric maze of strangers, intimidated by the streets and buildings" (1).

Only Chandler's self-reflexive *Playback* rivals McBain's penchant for smuggling clues from earlier episodes of the 87th into subsequent ones, thrilling literary detectives with a barrage of allusions, references, and even direct quotes.[14] No instalment would be complete, for instance, without stroke-of-a-pen *blazons* of the prime movers and shakers. Steve Carella, Meyer Meyer, Artie Brown, Bert Kling, Hal Willis, Cotton Hawes, Andy Parker, the 88th's Fat Ollie, and even the supporting cast have their set-piece blurbs reprinted almost verbatim from one book to the next. Fixing Ollie's girth, Meyer's bald pate, or Willis's short stature in the reader's eye, continuity is equally cultivated with the help of a myriad of subplots—from Kling's hapless romantic liaisons to the killing of Carella's father—which straddle consecutive novels.

Not even titles are immune to this high-gear wordplay. Coming right on the heels of *Money, Money, Money*, in *Fat Ollie's Book* Carella is heard to mutter: "Money, money, *money*" (51). Things get better still when, with his investigation going south, Carella seeks succour from a Florida attorney, Matthew Hope. The brief phone chat with the hero of McBain's "other" series—thirteen legal thrillers starring a Calusa, Florida advocate, Matthew Hope—gives both the feeling of a special bond between them. McBain's characters even go to see movies based on McBain's books. In *The Last Dance* the film was "part of a Kurosawa retrospective. It was titled *High and Low*, and it was based on a novel by an American who wrote cheap mysteries" (38). Quite.

All serials need to maintain continuity across time lapses between instalments which, in the case of the 87th, have been as long as two years. This is one reason why the flamboyant (though never intrusive) author interlaces the series with clues for readers keen to exercise their literary-detective talents. But the number of these intertextual stitches far exceeds the needs of a sequential narrative, even one diffused across half a century. The crucial reason for the stress on character continuity harks to McBain's narrative experiment which stunningly reverses the relation between people and places. Stories are typically driven by narrative agents who act against a more or less static background of their historical setting. Foregrounding character continuity and turning Carella et al. into fixed points on the story grid, instead, the author in effect recalibrates them into a stable backdrop on which to project his most dynamic and complex character—the City. After all, as he remarks in *Killer's Payoff*, "a city is only a collection of people and people are timeless" (1–2).

The 87th Precinct sits in the heart of a metropolis which, all concrete and realism on the one hand, is all personification and metaphor on the other. You may hate her for her slums and poverty but, as with the femme fatale, you cannot turn away from her charms. You may be drawn to her glitter and knockout skylines but hurry past ghettos like the black Diamondback, so full of roaches and crack vials even burglars do not bother any more. McBain's imagery is an anatomy of social contrast. One moment it's a 'burbs backyard filled with domestic bliss in the shape of crisp laundry hung out to dry. The next it's back to the rat race in the rat cage. As awe and veneration vie with garbage and gore, the City drives McBain's unique brand of artertainment, his own rhapsody in police blue. With the cops grinding out their shifts under the city's neon eyes, the narrator pays equal tribute to her chic and greed, both of them writ large and 200-proof American.

"2,000 street gangs, 4,000 minimalls,
20,000 sweatshops, and 100,000 homeless"
– Mike Davis (1998)

Larger even than its real-life correlative, the Big Bad City is a pulsing superbeing caught in the daily drama of living on the edge. From the ecological standpoint, a metropolitan sprawl is, of course, an aberration of human nature rather than optimal habitats for *Homo sapiens sapiens*. Overcrowded worse than municipal zoos, overrun by bipedal predators high on adrenalin not from flight but *fight* response, American conurbations could be mad-scientist experiments in urban sociology. As if on cue, in a 2000 interview McBain remarked: "I see the city in the 87th Precinct as being a metaphor for the entire world."[15]

Ranging from Dutch traders who in 1619 dumped the first cargo of slaves onto Jamestown's shores, to Saudi raiders who in 2001 obliterated the World Trade Centre, McBain metes narrative justice to the crown jewel of urban United States. In this city, as he puts it, *anything* could happen. And in between *Cop Hater* (1956) and *Fiddlers* (2005), with the investigative journalist's eye for detail, he patiently chronicles the days in the life of that dominant genus, the city-dweller. His cycle of blockbusters-with-gravitas follows the boom-and-bust cycle of New York City, measuring its greatness in the expanse from the penthouse to the subway grate. A single novel like *Mischief* stakes out a course in urban civics.

> ... the city had cut its hospital budget by thirty-five percent last year and the Chancery was a city hospital. It was now working with a skeleton staff more appropriate to a clinic in Zagreb than to a hospital in one of the world's largest and most influential cities. (44)

> Four out of five American families were caring at home for their sick or elderly parents. Women constituted seventy-five percent of these caretakers. (46)

> There were four million Alzheimer's sufferers in the United States of America. This number was expected to triple within the next twenty-five years. (47)

> One out of every four blacks in this city was foreign-born. (85)

> Nowadays, the immigrants you got from Latin America and the Caribbean preferred remaining citizens of their native lands, shuttling back and forth like diplomats between countries, supporting nuclear families here and extended families in their homelands. (86)

> Actually, nothing sold on the street was every *truly* pure; the more the drug was stepped on, the more profit there was for everyone down the line. But the new stuff was decidedly more potent than what the city's estimated 200, 000 heroin addicts were used to. (91)

> Crim Mis [Criminal Mischief] *One* was defined as: *With intent to do so and having no right to do so nor any reasonable ground to believe that one has such right, damaging property of another: 1. In an amount exceeding $1,500; OR 2. by means of an explosive.* (127)

… targeting a doctor who performed abortions, telephoning him and screaming the word "Murderer!" into his ear was considered a crime in most states of the union. In this state, it was called Aggravated Harassment, and it was a Class-A misdemeanor, punishable by the same year in prison and/or thousand dollar fine a graffiti writer could get for vandalizing a building. (131).

… simple Harassment, as opposed to the *aggravated* kind … was defined as 'engaging in a course of conduct or repeatedly committing acts which alarm or seriously annoy another person and which serve no legitimate purpose'. (132)

In this city, some twenty to thirty police officers were shot every year. (202).

… in the month of January … the precinct had dispatched Charlie Two to the [homeless men's] shelter a total of eight times, three of those times to investigate reported assaults, five of them to investigate emergencies that subsequently required hospitalization for rat bites and/or drug overdoses. (227)

In this city, killing someone wasn't such a big deal. In the first quarter of the year, for example, five hundred and forty-six murders were committed … Sixty-one percent of all the murders in this city were committed by firearms. (259)

Murder in the Second Degree, a Class-A felony defined in §125.15 with the words 'A person is guilty of murder in the second degree when, under circumstances evincing a depraved indifference to human life, he recklessly engages in conduct which creates a grave risk of death to another person, and thereby causes the death of another person. … Manslaughter in the Second Degree was defined in §125.15 as 'Recklessly causing the death of another person'. (349)

Granted the primacy of cliff-hanger investigation, there is much more to the urban procedural than crime. Raising awareness about the plight of hospitals, McBain is echoed by Senator Charles E. Schumer (New York): "Medicare budget cuts are slashing nearly $3.4 million a week from New York City hospitals." As the latter pointed out in the fiscal year 2002/03, "hospitals in the five boroughs stand to lose $175.9 million, with teaching hospitals in the area losing $98.1 million; hospital-based skilled nursing facilities losing $15 million this year; hospital-based home health associations losing $15 million; an overall reduction in scheduled payment inflation updates costing area hospitals an additional $15.7 million; and $32.2 million being lost in other reductions." No wonder, as McBain writes, that four out of five American families care at home for their sick and elderly. Forty two million citizens—more than the *metropolitan areas* of New York, Los Angeles, Detroit, Chicago, San Francisco, Atlanta and Baltimore combined—have no health coverage whatsoever.[16]

When the sound of gunfire in *The Big Bad City* 'hood is said to be as common as the sound of salsa, it might seem like a pulp-fiction conceit. But any notion of hyperbole and artistic license is again dispelled by facts which bear out the fiction.

In its own graphic way, *City Crime Rankings: Crime in Metropolitan America* makes no statistical bones about our space-age cities being breeding grounds for every class of wrong conceivable. From murder to forcible rape to motor vehicle theft, no one is safe any more—not even with one cop for every 370 people in the land (not counting hired security personnel who numerically outstrip the blues). The need for auxiliary security corps is so urgent, and their already prodigious numbers swelling so fast, that the line between private and public policing is getting distinctly fuzzy, giving a new twist to the old slang: "the fuzz."

Even as privatization of law enforcement (not to mention penitentiaries) continues to make headway, it is business as usual in the crime business. In 1995 "a crime occurred in the United States every two seconds" (9), to a total of almost 14 million *reported* offences. Of those, a little under 2 million were violent crimes. Put another way, murder, forcible rape, robbery, and aggravated assault "occurred every 18 seconds" (10) somewhere in the country. Not surprisingly, crime blighted the two heavyweights the most. The "baddest" of the class of 1995 was Los Angeles with a grand total of over half a million crimes, followed by the Big Apple with almost half a million, and Detroit with *only* a quarter million (rounded down). Statistically, crime and crowd went hand in hand. *Datapedia of the United States* put Las Vegas at the head of sixty American cities with "double-digit growth rates between 1980 and 1996" (4).

The link between crime and the city was memorably brought to the public by none other than J. Edgar Hoover in the 1964 public report, *Crime in the United States*. "When our national population was related to the volume of crime, a rate of 1,198 serious offences per 100,000 inhabitants was established. This was a 9 percent rise in the crime rate over 1962. Since 1958 crime has increased five times faster than our population growth" (3), hectored the FBI director. Thirty years later, fueled by worsening socio-economic conditions, the 1995 national crime rate was more than four times higher: 5,277 per 100,000. These same socio-economic conditions were exacerbated by the continued migration of "the other half" into inner city cores, and the haemorrhage of affluence into the suburban ring. Both were shaping that archetypal 20th-century urban phenomenon: a megalopolis patrolled by the increasingly defeasible "magalopolice".

Speaking of vice and men, McBain points out that while the police win some battles, they are losing the war, unable to stem the groundswell of crime rooted in social and economic neglect too acute for any precinct to deal with. Nor is he shy to figure racism, ill-masked by a façade of political correctness, as the reason why tens of millions of Americans cannot emancipate themselves from the quicksand of poverty. As in real-life New York, his fictive ghettoes and slums are better known by their ethnic monikers than the white-washed names tacked on by developers. The lack of integration simmers to the surface every time US citizens are treated as Americans in name only—especially when their heritage gives a lie to the WASP cookie-cutter (McBain's own name change is a case in point). The proliferation of these hyphenated Americans, as his cops never tire of pointing out, is a constant reminder of the mental apartheid that permeates the land.[17]

McBain's procedurals make clear that racial wars are fought today with the same desperation as in the post-emancipation decades in which Negroes were sold down the river of Yankee capitalism. They do not hide that, in this game of cutthroat chess, every move by the White is countered by the Black. Up here, in *The Big Bad City*, "there isn't even a pretense of races mingling. In the South, you don't have to sit in the back of a bus anymore and you don't have to drink at separate water fountains, but at the same time you don't see any pepper-and-salt couples ... They don't *say* nigger anymore, but they still *think* nigger. Same as up here. The *N* word is forbidden, but that doesn't stop the white man from thinking it. The only reason he doesn't say it out loud is he knows it can get him killed" (197).

Part of his crash course in racial civics, McBain's dollops of ethnic realism make even more sense when set in the context of who is working and who is not. By the late 1990s, during the Clinton era of economic expansion, national unemployment was whittled down to roughly 5 percent, but the rate masks serious disparities. Among blacks 16 to 19 years old—the age group most likely to strike out in all senses of the word—the unemployment rate topped 27 percent, and among all black males 16 percent.[18] The news, of course, is hardly newsworthy. From 1947 to 1998, in a half-century no different from those that preceded it, the unemployment rates for black men and women have consistently dwarfed the national average and those of their white counterparts.

Thanks to an almost Spartan parsimony of expression, McBain can boil down a century of urban life to a paragraph or two. F. Scott Fitzgerald and Nelson DeMille needed full-scale novels, *The Great Gatsby* and *Gold Coast*, to capture the heart of the Long Island aristocracy. McBain time-lapses it into a snapshot of the housing and social development in his fictional suburb of "Sand's Spit." As for Manhattan/Isola itself, *Kiss* says it all. "This was a city in decline. The cabbie knew it because he drove all over this city and saw every part of it. Saw the strewn garbage and the torn mattresses and the plastic debris littering the grassy slopes of every highway, saw the bomb-crater potholes on distant streets, saw public phone booths without phones, saw public parks without benches, their slats torn up and carried away to burn, heard the homeless ranting or pleading or crying for mercy, heard the ambulance sirens and the police sirens day and night but never when you needed one, heard it all, and saw it all, and knew it all, and just rode on by" (147–8).

If every crime has a price, it's always bargain season in the American city, and one urban procedural, multiplied over millions of copies bought and read, weighs heavier than a bunch of promo flyers from NYC's Tourist Board. McBain is, of course, too seasoned an artist to turn his cycle into a litany of the United States' social ills. Good fiction is, after all, much more than a social document, no matter how pointed its facts of life. Even as he dispenses urban grit with both fists, the bestselling author never allows it to jolt the story out of the bullet-fast lane. Another proceduralist of a more forensic bent, Kathy Reichs, demurred in a 2000 interview: "The fact is that my books are good old fashioned murder mysteries." There's no better way to describe the 87th Precinct and its *dramatis personae* even as they search for social justice.

"We all have some bad in us, some ugliness, some good"
– Sergio Leone (1967)

John Douglas, a legendary FBI profiler and author, had no doubt why audiences continue to be spellbound by police procedurals. The procedural "allows the reader a window into a world that he or she may know nothing about. For example, the technique of the detective, whether it's an FBI agent, a policeman, or a journalist." Indeed, top practitioners of the art, such as Joseph Wambaugh, Martin Cruz-Smith, Jeffrey Deaver or Donald Harstad, lace their plots with the minutiae of police science and police bureaucracy. No longer Chandleresque knights, their case detectives and lab techs follow the same rulebook as the cops who get star-billing on a mounting number of nonfiction hit-shows, such as *Medical Detectives, The New Detectives, The FBI Files, America's Most Wanted, Exhibit A, Cold Case Files,* or *American Justice.*

The spirit of realism is so overwhelming that Douglas openly identifies his procedurals (co-authored with Mark Olshaker) as vehicles for educating the public on how to prevent crime. "One of the things which I think we tried to do in *Journey into Darkness* and then again to some extent in *Obsession,* is we've tried to make children into profilers themselves. I mean, if they're going to avoid being victims, they've got to understand what it is they can do. If a child is lost in a shopping mall, that child has to become a profiler and say, 'Who can you trust?' And we tell them to look for certain types of people. You look for people in uniform. You look for people with name tags. You look for people behind counters. You look for pregnant women or women with other children. To merely tell a kid not to talk to strangers is not going to be very helpful. In fact, it's going to be very detrimental. If a kid gets lost in a shopping mall, he's got nobody to talk to but strangers."

But if realism is the name of the game, McBain goes one better again by *visually* integrating the procedural routine into his books. From teletype messages, missing person's reports, crime scene sketches, fingerprint files, case reports, rap sheets, search warrants, scene-of-crime reports, laboratory reports, autopsy reports, surveillance reports, complaint reports, evidence tags, age and gender tables, bomb diagrams, bullet casings, pistol licences, duty grids, toxicology charts, down to search warrant applications, interrogation transcripts, and sections of the penal code, generations of readers get to *see* what lies behind the thin blue line. Book by book, the 87th Precinct faithfully reproduces the daily grind of a forensic administrative machine.

McBain's early procedurals laid down the ground-rules of the then novel genre. As time went on, however, the ambitious writer began to bend the very rules he had invented. His progression from the police to the urban procedural occasionally surfaces in the "catch-me-if-you-can" asides aimed at his many imitators. Thus Fat Ollie Weeks, the cycle's top-notch crime buster (and top-notch bigot) gets to write a perfectly awful book about cops in *Fat Ollie's Book*. "The trouble was he was trying too much to sound like all those pissant writers out there who were not cops but who were writing what they called 'police procedurals'" (24), mocked his creator. Acclaimed artists who turn to fictive crime are, of course, as common as bread in a prison meatloaf. Even more than Borges or Eco, in the context the best example may be Akira Kurosawa whose legendary *High and Low* (1963) is a scene-by-scene adaptation of McBain's *King's Ransom* (1959), with Tokyo subbing as the urban jungle of the NYC.

The same realism characterizes his cops who span the gamut from good to bad to ugly. Some are chronically overworked family men, some lazy nine-to-fivers, and some, like Fat Ollie, are First Grade detectives and first-grade jerks. In *The Big Bad City*, for example, the big bad cop wastes no time proving himself bigot supreme. "The first thing Ollie always did with a Pakistani cab driver—or for that matter, any cab driver who looked like a fucking foreigner, which was only every other cab driver in the city—was show his shield. This was so there'd be no heated arguments later on; some of these fuckin camel jockeys were very sensitive" (266).

Even though McBain aims for mimetic justice, he is the first to concede that his detectives are ideals whose counterparts may be hard to find on New York City's payroll. "I know that all cops are not sterling characters. But you have to have someone to root for. I balance it with rotten cops who will take a bribe, who will beat somebody up."[19] Life, in this case, imitates art imitates life. Like Mark Fuhrman of the O. J. Simpson's murder-trial ill-fame, Fat Ollie is a top-dog investigator and a flaming racist who epitomizes the attitudes of many sworn officers of the law. In return, the attitudes of the public are evident in the abundance of "pig" jokes and other epithets hurled at the men and women supposed to protect them. In *The Big Bad City*, Carella sets Brown straight: "People don't like cops, is what it is. We remind them of storm troopers" (66).

All too often seen as coffee-and-donut caricatures at best, corrupt and trigger-happy brutes at worst, policemen and even whole departments have been sued for their real and imagined failures. Far from improving protection and making cops more accountable, it only closes the ranks and makes covering one's ass that much more of a priority. The fact that the police wield so much power, enforced by firearms, nightsticks, stun guns, Kevlar vests, and a code of silence grimmer than the omerta, is disconcerting to most citizens. Weighing the evidence on the prosecution and defence's sides, McBain points out that even as cops are distrusted, they get called to the front line whenever social bonds of civility slip.

Thrust into the limelight by the Frank Serpico, Rodney King and John Orr affairs, they will never be media darlings unless they overcome the image of incompetence, brutality, and abuse of power conjured up on TV and Hollywood blockbusters.

No picture of McBain's procedurals and cops would be complete without the women in blue. Of the female protagonists that enter and exit the series' inner core, Sharyn Cooke in particular underscores the difficulties women face with advancement in a male-dominated force. She first joins the cast in *Mischief* as a surgeon operating on a shot cop—another policewoman. She then lands a bigger role in *Romance* as Kling's girlfriend. By *Last Dance* (1999), Chief Cooke's rank and personal history have become as familiar as Kling's, and her relationship with him as fraught with interracial epiphany. "The unfortunate spelling of Sharyn's first name was due to the fact that her then thirteen-year-old, unwed mother didn't know how to spell Sharon. This same mother later put her through college and then medical school on money earned scrubbing floors in white men's offices after dark. Sharyn Cooke was black, the first woman of color ever appointed to the job she now held" (156).

How does McBain's fiction stack up against real life? Historically women were barred from the force until Alice Wells, the first American policewoman, joined the LAPD in 1910. Although by 1917 some thirty US cities employed women cops, they were for the most part entrusted only with desk duties and low-echelon public relations jobs. It was not until the Civil Rights Act (1964) and the Equal Employment Opportunity Act (1972) that women and minorities began to assume a more professional profile in policing. Rome was not, however, built in a day. In most departments today "activities associated with femininity are viewed as lower in status and further away from real police work than those linked to masculinity. Thus, the informal world of the street, clean money, normal violence, and routine lying are linked to masculinity and the police occupation. The academy and assorted 'inside' jobs involving secretarial and administrative tasks are perceived as feminine."[20]

The *Encyclopedia of Women and Crime* reports that nearly 80 percent of police units in the United States still have no women of colour in executive ranks, although some have indeed risen to deputy commissioner and commander in Pittsburgh, the District of Columbia, New York City, Philadelphia, Miami-Dade, and Detroit. In "Police Organizations, Municipal and State", Michelle Meloy finds that even when women "are successful at entering the profession, their upward mobility within law enforcement is likely to be curtailed ... [as] the overall token status of policewomen subjects them to gender stereotyping, increased job performance pressure, and isolation from male officers" (172). According to the US Department of Justice, in the year 2000 there were 800,000 full-time law enforcement officers across the United States, 100,000 of them women. Twelve percent plus does not sound like much, especially side by side with Britain's eighteen, but given the historical obstacles, it is not to be shrugged off lightly.[21]

Far from an escapist and violent mass-market product, the crime-and-vice procedural is a modern incarnation of naturalism in American letters, with Crane's *Maggie: A Girl of the Streets* and Dreiser's *Sister Carrie* at its roots. While postmodern aesthetics downplays reality as a simulacrum and narrative realism as passé, in McBain's hands popular art metes out justice to problems that beset four of every five of us. With ethnographic acumen second to none, he steals the show from other litterateurs whose offerings—of which Paul Auster's *New York Trilogy* may be best known—are long on self-deconstruction but short on crime and the city. "I consider the 87th Precinct a continuing novel about crime and punishment in our times, and each separate novel is like a chapter in a long, long novel," acknowledged the author in 1983.[22] Chronicling the quotidian rhythms of the City, the 87th's cycle refines the procedural into the winning recipe of knockout suspense and a survival manual for all urban dwellers.

In *The Age of Reform* (1956), Richard Hofstadter distilled four hundred years of American history into the observation that the United States was born in the country and has moved to the city. Today violent crime, urban blight, racial strife, chronic unemployment, ghetto housing, gangland streets, snarled traffic, civic graft, red-tape corruption, and dropout education are the reasons why affluent America in droves leaves the *urbs* for the suburbs. But for those who want to keep their hands on the pulse of the megalopolitan sprawl, the police mystery is often their best bet. And the fact that so many turn to it with a devotion which baffles pulp fiction critics is one more reason for according it critical attention and respect. For, even as they entertain, just like legal procedurals McBain's urban procedurals inform—and in some cases perhaps even form—the perceptions and values of tens of millions of readers.[23]

From the fact that McBain's procedurals are perfect beach books for intellectuals, it does not follow that they are minor literature. And from the fact that they are fiction, it does not follow that they are not to be taken as serious chronicles of America and its city blights. Today's urban habitat is not only the most prevalent, but the most complex historically, and McBain's procedurals are some of the best (not to say most readable) commentaries on its stresses and excesses. But don't take anyone's word for it. Settle the matter for yourself, even at the risk of finding that his City is like the bottom of your shoe—once you get going, it will follow you everywhere.

CHAPTER 4

Just Apassin' Through:

BETTERMENT AND ITS DISCONTENTS IN AMERICA'S LITERATURE OF THE ROAD

Earle Waugh

> *"Old elephants limp off to the hills to die;*
> *old Americans go out to the highway*
> *and drive themselves to death with huge cars."*
> – Hunter S. Thompson, *Fear and Loathing in Las Vegas*

Of all the symbols of conquest of the American landscape, the road seems to occupy a special place. More than anything else, it appears to capture and express the immediacy of American civilization's victory over the unruly continent. And yet, instead of a simple apotheosis of this victory, literature about the road is replete with condemnations, hand-wringing and conflict. In this chapter, I want to examine the road as a kind of refracted American identity, as a prism indicative of basic American values, precisely because the road is capable of encompassing and representing so many themes. In an analysis drawn largely from America's literary works, great and small, I contend that the conundrums of American self-identity have from the very start had to deal with the weighted notion of *betterment*. The term, as I see it, hides aesthetic, moral and religious elements. The drive to betterment has pushed the nation to constant self-appraisal, redefinition and concern with its growth, some of which have found their way into important representations of the road and the road's destiny—the city.

In its most compelling instances, the road genre has left a legacy of tension and, in some cases, a noticeable ambiguity concerning views of American identity. In this sense, of course, the road parallels the city for, especially in the early days of America, the construction of the City was the goal of all those who pushed roads into the wilderness. I explore this prismatic character of the road in four interlocking segments. The first, "Writing the Troubling Road," looks at the writers who depict American sensitivities to the early notions of betterment. Here roads appear as stepping-stones to new cities and economic possession of the continent. As civilization moved out across the continent, defining American destiny took on the role of a national agenda, expressed in carving out tracts into the frontier wilderness. Hence I critique this agenda, trying to grasp the purpose of America beyond construction of its roads and buildings.

In the second segment, "Conflicted Theory: City/Road/People," I move to a more theory-laden view of the city, insofar as it has been used to provide justification for the road system. Out of this comes a wider perspective: at some point, the development of transportation corridors and linkages between cities becomes symbolic of the Yankee victory over the physical expanse of the continent. Thus paving America's corridors reflects the American can-do spirit—its ultimate expression being the massive Interstate Highway System. Here, for all to see, was a very physical representation of betterment. And yet, scarcely had this brainchild of President Eisenhower's got underway, than trouble began. I examine how American writers wrestled with the problematic of the city: the metropolis and its roads in tension with their very raison d'être ... the people.

By the mid-twentieth century, the tensions within the American dream begin to boil over, not in some bucolic glen in Ohio or California, but in the mega-city itself. The great social issue of whether roads can trump people indicates a refined sense of betterment in operation; and yet, to counter this positive theme, it became clear that the construction and functioning of the modern American city is largely disconnected from the will of its inhabitants. Alienation set in. The old Southern spiritual, "*This world is not my home, I'm just apassin' through*," became an anthem of disengagement with the here-and-now of American social politics.

By the time we get to the postindustrial times and postmodernist writers, the roads have taken on distinctive and sometimes menacing qualities. Betterment is now a highly contested term. Hence the next segment, "Motoring into Crisis: Road Triumph, Street Anguish, and the New Romantic Road," focuses on the ways in which betterment is perceived in the conflicted environment of today. It throws in relief a number of conservative attempts to impose betterment—if such a thing were even possible—in the United States or around the world. Seeking to find a network within the maze of roads, or a community in disconnected groupings of the like-minded, writers demonstrate how the American spirit chaffs and then cuts loose from engaging with the political culture of the country. Finally, in "Writer's Denouement," I highlight two directions in which the betterment theme seems to be moving today, in the midst of ambiguity and discontent of the twenty-first century.

Writing the Troubling Road

Founder and long-time editor of *Landscape* magazine, J. B. Jackson, commented aptly: "One of the least investigated aspects of our European-American culture is our ambivalent attitude toward the road" (5). There are all sorts of reasons why ordinary Americans might look at the road askance. Every day a good number are tied up for hours in traffic jams, and a frightful number every year are maimed or killed.[1] Yet, Hunter Thompson's epigraph from the chapter header notwithstanding, it is not only the old who take to the road with a vengeance. It is clear that the experience of getting one's first car has taken on all the elements of an American rite of passage.[2] At least some pop culture connotations of the road are connected to coming of age, and a jaunt to the local Lover's Lookout (in a snazzy car, natch!) is the trysting-place of choice for first sexual encounters— look no further than Jim Jacobs and Warren Casey's *Grease.*

Beyond these cultural expressions, wheels are a mixed image ... they can be a symbol of everything from blinding wealth (*The Great Gatsby*) to absolute machismo (*Easy Rider*). Even such beauty as a parkway is not without its hooks: roads make enchanting and remote places, such as Rockefeller's Acadia National Park, accessible to everyone to visit and trample. The other side of the freedom the road brings turns out to be, inevitably, the policy conflict between preserving wilderness and making it available to the public.

Ambiguity over what roads bring is nothing new. Consider these lines from a love poem of a young woman meeting her beloved prince Mehy on the road in ancient Egypt:

> I decided to go to Nefrusy/ And while I was staying there
> I came across Mehy in his chariot on the road with his buddies.
> I did not know whether to avoid him or pass by, nonchalant-like ...
> My heart is clueless: "Why should you pass by Mehy?"
> If I stroll past him/I would blurt out my moves (feelings)
> "Look I am yours!" I will say to him/Then he will shout out my name
> And assign me to the mess of the first one in his entourage.[3]

Because roads are connections not between cities but people, we are compelled to recognize the presence of what Graham Greene called "the human factor"— with the inevitable complexities that it implies—that makes the role of roads in American culture so troubling ... if the young Egyptian woman's experience is anything to go by, roads are ineluctable expressions of the human psyche. From very early on, even in very primitive social situations, roads have not been mere functional conduits for traders and goods, but part of the very apparatus of existence. As in the young woman and Mehy's case, roads have the potential to be the theatre of intense personal desire and great individual loss.

Philosophers, social theorists, and writers of all sorts have noted how roads construct people and mediate issues of the heart, as much as they orient cities and found empires. Roads, if you like, are the wrappers of civilization. Not incidentally, the great American philosopher Ralph Waldo Emerson insisted that some kind of civility always came with the road. "Where the Indian trail gets widened, graded, and bridged to a good road," he wrote, "there is a benefactor, there is a missionary, a pacificator, a wealth-bringer, a maker of markets, a vent for industry" (9). In effect, the road is a cultural marker. It declares the civil shaping of the country's landscape. It provides the medium through which development, social life and polity are activated. And more than most cultures, America's vision of itself is embraced, mapped and etched by the road.

And yet, J. B. Jackson was surely on to something ... like most cultures, Americans, too, are troubled by roads. Ordinarily, it is difficult to see what the problem may be, so automatic is our expectation of their ultimate utility in transportation, their pragmatic functioning essential to our livelihood. Still, the very ease of access from any one place in America to another comes with a moral impact and a latent price. What has been destroyed to provide this asphalted ease? What toll has been exacted for this freedom of movement? What natural environment has been destroyed for this fleeting passage of people and goods?

My awareness of this moral confrontation arose out of work on Roger Vandersteene.[4] A Hemingway-type priest, who toiled out his life in Indigenous outposts in northern Alberta, Vandersteene was a poet and an artist. He struggled mightily with the impact of white culture among his charges, dying too early, when cancer overthrew his labors. In writing about his life, I read what he had to say about the building of roads in an unpublished book called *And They Built Roads.* Vandersteene unequivocally condemned white society for constructing roads into remote reservations on the pretext of making it easier to provide supplies. In reality, he insisted, the road was nothing but a tool of assimilation and destruction ... Aboriginal youngsters would travel to town, to the underside of life, to drugs, prostitution and ultimately death. They could not cope with the cultural dimensions of the road and "the Big Bad City"—as Ed McBain calls it—that often lay at its end.

This was my first-hand encounter with the conflicted nature of the road. But, I had to remind myself, Vandersteene's experience had taken place in the northern wildernesses of Canada. How much of the same attitude and the same misery had prevailed in the urbanized and highway-routed United States? What price had the United States of America paid for punching roads across Indigenous lands, through gorgeous vistas that were no longer so gorgeous when split by asphalt? Was this long-submerged moral condemnation the source of its inner conflicts?

Religious Shaping of the Landscape

Older students of America had concluded that the nation had been built upon a kind of sacred trust that had been fundamentally broken—a trust that began with the Puritans of the Massachusetts Bay Company, who had laid the foundations for an American consciousness and a sacred responsibility to nature. More than forty years ago, the celebrated literary historian Perry Miller took stock of that consciousness and responsibility in *Errand in the Wilderness*, setting the New England sense of nature against the founding of cities:

In various ways—not often agreeing among themselves—they identified the health, the very personality, of America with Nature, and therefore set it in opposition to the concepts of the city, the railroad, the steamboat. This definition of the fundamental issue of life in America became that around which Thoreau, Melville, and Whitman organized their peculiar expression. They ... present us with the problem of American self-recognition as being essentially an irreconcilable opposition between Nature and civilization— which is to say between forest and town, spontaneity and calculation, heart and head, the unconscious and the self-conscious, the innocent and the debauched. (207–8)

Miller observed that the founding of New England by religious conservatives had had an impact on its subsequent cultural forms. The "Separatist Christian" ideology of the Puritans had shaped many of the new nations' expectations of itself. Miller's perception of American history stands, however, in counterpoint to the well-known "frontier thesis" of the historian, Frederick Jackson Turner. In his 1893 classic, *The Frontier in American History,* Turner had identified the openness and challenge of the apparently limitless empty forest as a progenitor of American democracy, linking the latter to the westward quest to move and conquer that lingers in the American psyche. Even though Turner's notions have been dismissed as far too sweeping to account for the phenomena he tackled, they have undeniably continued to play a role at the popular level, as in Kennedy's rallying depiction of the Cold War space race as America's New Frontier.

Indeed, Miller found too many tensions within America to accept such a monolithic conception of its history. He looked rather to the immediate experience of America within the Puritan mindset, and saw it constantly troubled by the goal of creating a new and blessed land while trying to remain responsible to God for the beautiful terrain divinity had bequeathed. In his view, some kind of pact with God, a covenant, had gone badly wrong, and ever since Americans have had to deal with the ensuing moral and environmental headache. Indeed today, the religious right finds itself in an unprecedented alliance with the progressive left when it comes to concerns about the destruction of environment, regarded by Christian groups as God-given.

Certainly the tensions between the wholesale development of America and its guilt at despoiling the land accounts for many of the conflicted themes even in the earliest New World literature. The fact is that, even if the Puritans saw the peopling of the new continent as a mission placed upon them by the divine decree—and saw the fruits from America's abundant natural storehouse as a yardstick of His benevolent approval—the later-comers may well not have shared this vision of American life. Somewhere along the road there has been a severance from the sacred trust.

In 1609, Robert Gray published a tourist/immigration promo-document, *A Good Speed to Virginia,* in which he distinguished how the inhabitants of the new land were to be understood. "The earth ... which is man's fee-simple by deeds of gift of God, is the greater part of it possessed and wrongfully usurped by wild beasts, and unreasonable creatures, or by brutish savages, which by reason of their godless ignorance, and blasphemous idolatrie, are worse than those beasts which are a most wild and savage nature."[5] What he neglected to mention was that some of the world's biggest and greatest cities, such as Cahokia (or indeed any number of Meso-American cities), had thrived before the Europeans arrived. Furthermore, it was these same "savages" who taught the newcomers how to survive and prosper within the new ecology. As Herbert Aptheker points out: "The trails of the Indians were the paths of the colonists (as so many of them were to become the roads of the automobile age). In a word, the Indians taught the Europeans how to live in the New World, and were repaid by having that World taken away from them" (20).[6]

This Indigenous phase of encounter with America may have been lost forever. Outside tribal stories, local memories, and perhaps Howard Zinn's revisionary *A People's History of the United States* (1995), the official histories available to us systematically fail to remember them. Maybe the moral is to be found in Tom Robbins's *Even Cowgirls Get the Blues*, in the words of one of his characters, the Chink, spoken from the perspective of "alternative-culture" observer. "Technology shapes psyches as well as environments, and maybe the peoples of the West are too sophisticated, too permanently alienated from Nature to make use of their pagan heritage" (234). Maybe. Or maybe a kind of preferred forgetfulness lies at the heart of American development. Whichever the case, something has indeed become irretrievably lost when the Aboriginal trails were upgraded into roads even before the political birth of the United States of America, and a haunting void that cannot be filled was stitched into the continental fabric.

Benevolent Beginning: The American City as a New Jerusalem

If "Indian" roads were a benevolent means by which newly arrived Americans first moved into the hinterland, the end point of these roads was the ideal New England city which took on quite a religious coloring. This became particularly apparent during the brief but fervent period of religious revival, known as the Great Awakening. In 1697 and then again in 1716, Cotton Mather wrote of his hopes that Boston would become the New Jerusalem, while Jonathan Edwards preached the Great Awakening as a "dawning, or at least a prelude to the millennium."[7] The writings of Mather and Edwards helped to promote a type of landscape piety, a hallowing of space and road. An articulate preacher and shrewd political leader, Cotton Mather was certainly a prominent exponent of the "natural" in New England. Certain that the distraught state of the territory's history could be gleaned from Biblical events, in *Days of Humiliation* he directed his listeners' attention to Isaiah 3:26, and the prophecy that outlined the fate of the Daughters of Zion:

> *When Zion was desolate,* by the Roman Conquest, (unto which this prophecy might extend) there were Coins made in Commemoration of the Conquest, and on those Coins there was a Remarkable Exposition of this Prophecy. On the Reverse of those Medals, which are to be seen unto the Day, there is, *A Silent Woman sitting upon the Ground, and leaning against a Palm-tree, with this Inscription* IUDAEA CAPTA. Nor was any Conquered City or Country, before this if *Judaea*, ever thus draw upon Medals, as, *A Woman sitting upon the Ground.* Alas, if poor *New-England*, were to be thrown upon her old Coin, we might show her *Leaning* against her Thunderstruck *Pine Tree, Desolate, sitting upon the Ground.* Ah! *New England!* Upon how many accounts, mayst thou say with her in Ruth 1:13. *The Hand of the Lord is gone out against me!* (8)

In effect, so confident was Mather that America offered God's opportunity for its New People, that he deliberately blended Israel's ancient story into his New England ideology. Rank claims for land and more land were couched in thundering "wilderness of Sinai" language. Thus, when the colonialists were jointly attacked by the French and Indigenous warriors in 1690, it was natural that the following remarks of his would became widely published and disseminated as *On the Necessities and Advantages of a Public Spirit:*

> We are Precipitated into such Destress and Danger, as we have never been before: Nothing so Exquisite has hitherto befallen us. Our cause indeed is That, in Math. 3:10 *The Ax is laid unto the Roots of the Trees*: The Knife of our God has been heretofore cutting and Pruning of us, but either *Ill Fruit* or *No Fruit* is the *Best Fruit* which we have hitherto yielded unto that glorious Husbandman. Wherefore He is now come forth against us, with an *Ax*, a French *Ax*, accompanied by *Indian Hatchets*; and our very Root is like to receive the strokes thereof ... with an eye to the Execution of the Sentence upon the Jewes, we find mentioned in Isai.66.6: *A Voice from the City, a Voice from the Temple, a Voice from the Lord.* (33–34)

In Mather's perception, the center of true social guidance arose out of the city, God's city, Isaiah's Jerusalem ... and he continued at great length to demonstrate that the same state of affairs obtained in New England. Such language, let us remember, was widespread throughout the fledgling colonies, providing a religious and literary framework for the developing nation's conscience about what its larger task was to be. Cities, in short, were to be jewels in the crown of the consecrated continent.

Mather's counterpart in the Great Awakening was Jonathan Edwards, regarded as early America's greatest theologian. Edwards's philosophy led him to argue, among other things, that heaven as a city is "represented by various similitudes, so as to suit to the disposition of everyone. There is nothing that is esteemed highly by men, that is not sinful, but what the glories of heaven are likened to."[8] He furthermore developed a whole theory of natural order, wherein he insists that "there are some things that the natural man perceiveth not and that he neither can know as long as he continues a natural man and that are discerned no other way but spiritually." Nevertheless, even in the same volume, he views the natural order—to be understood as the New England colonial culture—mainly as a vehicle to the supernatural, and natural and temporal things as (somewhat Platonically) shadows of spiritual and eternal realities.

In *One Whole and Happy Society* (1992), Jerald R. McDermott argued that Edwards saw America in terms of a national covenant with God. The New World was interpreted through the Christian imagery of a "City on the Hill" (Matthew 5:14), with all roads leading into it. The land of plenty was a social expression of God's blessing to the faithful. Conversely, when evil befell, it was interpreted as evidence of America's perfidy. It is no secret that this idyllic vision of the relationship between the natural city on earth and the heavenly City of God rested on the theology of St. Augustine. Like the medieval theologian, Edwards, too, insisted that the true City of God was not of this world. And yet, he argued that the covenant with God gave some cities greater exposure to the divine light, as evidenced by the fact that New England had been "glutted" by the gospel through the "Great Awakening" and its greater "civil liberties."[9]

Edwards directly connected the Great Awakening to the widespread belief in God's plan for a golden age (or millennium) in America. His teachings had influenced many preachers and public figures, especially when it came to the War of Independence and the conception of the "manifest destiny," and while opinions differ over the impact of his millenialism on American identity, it is widely acknowledged as crucial for the growth of American civil religion.[10] Many of Edwards's notions echo, in fact, throughout the modern times, not only in literature of the city but also philosophy. His arresting sermons affected not only his peers but, almost two hundred years later, one of America's greatest philosophical studies of religion, William James's *Varieties of Religious Experience* (1902). Indeed, it is frequently forgotten that Edwards's *A Faithful Narrative of the Surprising Work of God* (1738) is not only a celebration of spiritual reawakening, but of the empiricism of John Locke as well.[11]

Creative Road Identity: Other Literary Models

However much the founding fathers adopted the Christian models for the new land, and envisioned their way through the wilderness in terms of God leading Israelites to Canaan, the fact is that the journey between the cities they founded was all-too-human in complexion. Herein lies the source of another view of the road in early American travel narratives. Sarah Kemble Knight—who might well have sat under the tutelage of Cotton Mather—was an unknown Boston shop-owner, an enterprise she continued after her marriage. In 1704 she set out alone from Boston to New Haven to settle the estate of a relative, Caleb Trowbridge. In its wake she left us a unique account of her journey, detailing every day's happenings before retiring to bed. Historically, the five days she spent on the road took place in the same decade as Benjamin Franklin's birth ... and the 1704 roads—routes of the postal riders, really—were by all accounts very primitive.

Edward Tylor, a Puritan minister-poet, portrayed the fears of travel through the American wilderness in almost apocalyptic terms, but Kemble Knight did not use his type of imagery. Instead, she opted to look back a century to the Elizabethan romances of Emanuel Forde. She wrote in her diary:

> Thus Jogging on with an easy pace, my Guide telling mee it was dangero's to Ride hard in the Night, (whch his horse had the sence to avoid,) Hee entertained me with the Adventurs he had passed by late Rideing, and eminent Dangers he had escaped, so that, Remembering the Hero's in Parismus and the Knight of the Oracle, I didn't know but I had mett wth a Prince diguis'd. When we had Ridd about an how'r, wee come into a thick swamp, wch. by Reason of a great fogg, very much startled mee, it being now very Dark. But nothing dismay'd John: Hee had encountered a thousand and a thousand such Swamps, having a Universall Knowledge in the woods; and readily Answered all my inquiries wch. were not a few.[12]

Such, in short, were the physical roads of the colonies. Travelers like Madame Knight regularly had to face the vagaries of the terrain, fording rivers, losing horses to the taxing passes, riding hard to escape the loss of sunlight, and dealing with floods, overflowing streams and rockslides, to say nothing of hostelries and wayside inns crammed with drinkers and revelers. The roads were almost unremittingly wild, dreary, and melancholy, so much so that their reality was pungently expressed by a contemporary of Knight: "Good roads are like angel's visits, few and far between."[13] Indeed, it was no revelation that roads were uniformly terrible. By 1752 the number of people trying to move into Carolina, for instance, turned into a flood—Scotch-Irish, Germans, Welsh, thousands upon thousands of them forced to use the Great Philadelphia Wagon Road, better known as simply "The Bad Road."[14] It was shortly thereafter, therefore, that states began the arduous task of improving the links among the growing colonial cities ... and the paving of America began.

Given the early state of the roads, it is instructive that for the early writers neither the terrain nor the journey was described as unknown or untried. They were modeled, instead, after previous depictions of journeys in quite different literary cultures. In effect, the New World experience was framed by an authoritative literature from afar ... by scriptures in the case of the religious, or by European literary heritage in the case of the educated. In that way, travel was connected to the road—and the road to the city—through another time and place, making it more "literary" and familiar, and thus more acceptable. Literature and the act of writing, if you will, helped Americans feel less like Elizabeth Ashbridge, another American traveler who described herself as a "stranger in a strange land" (in another allusion to the Old Testament).

Once the building of roads began, the very use of the term "wild" had to be curbed. The roads were no longer isolated, bereft of traffic, or threatening, since travelers—who were often immigrants to the New World—grouped together to better weather the road. Travel around America of that era often turned into a truly social occasion, albeit always tinged with adventure. Starting in the mid-eighteenth century, then, the cultural meaning of roads has been very quickly added to the totality of American colonial experience. In fact, Frederick Jackson Turner's very depiction of America as a frontier—that is, an environment whose outer borders open onto savage, free land—was a constructed myth to deny the existence of any people in the interior of the continent, and to encourage the entrepreneur to open a trail into that emptiness.[15]

In effect, the early American experience *had* to be conflicted, rooted as it was in its European (mostly British) intellectual legacy on the one hand, and in the religious tradition on the other. Not surprisingly, then, the early colonists took two parallel literary roads to depict the American city and its links to the road, one drawn from European literature and the other rooted in Biblical imagery. Yet both are ambivalent by their very character ... one deriving from a history of an old, multi-stated culture, the other arising out of the creative interpretation of Biblical models, even more ancient and geographically remote than the European states. Neither precedent fits well with what was on the ground.

No matter. American ideology was now firmly rooted in a sense of collective betterment. The colonists immediately began to re-shape and merge these parallel tracks into distinctively American perceptions and mythologies, largely because of the social and religious pressures in the settlements. Thus New England's millennial sentiment, which migrated into a wide variety of American writings, was derived basically from the "home-made" revivals and awakenings of the early days. Oddly enough, these experiences gave Americans a sense of distinctive calling, of Godly import, one dimension of which transmutes into the physical compass of the conquering road. What is left behind, or even buried out of sight, is the fact that the road (or soon enough the iron horse) sweeps over someone else's territory. Hence, this kind of betterment comes with a buried price and, at one and the same time, roads become the symbol of the burgeoning America and its extension of European culture.

Returning to Miller for a moment, it must be said that, despite the attractiveness of his ideas, the conflict between nature and civilization cannot carry the whole freight of conflict within America's attitude to the roads and the landscape. The reason is quite simple. These same themes have been rehearsed over and over from the time of Samuel Danforth in the seventeenth century, through Jonathan Edwards in the eighteenth, through the master of America's landscape painting, and Thomas Cole, in the nineteenth, right down to the ecologists of today. Had these visions of the primacy of Nature really taken root in the American psyche, one would have thought it would have made a profound impact by now. None, however, seems to have had much success in curbing the empire's pragmatic conquest. Nor can this antagonism between nature and culture explain why the car has been such a triumph in America, despite the huge cost to the environment acknowledged even by the current President (an "oiler," nonetheless) in his 2006 State of the Union address.

Thus the early period in America reflects moral tensions between the physical growth of America at the expense of America's primitive beauty; between the crucial presence of the First Nations and their largely ignored contribution to America's expansion; and between the Christian religious and European literary models of roads and their experiences. Despite these, the moral sense of betterment urges the soon-to-be new nation to the physical control of the continent and occupation of its space through immigrant-constructed-and-peopled cities. Roads, then, were the means to link the symbols of American transformation—the cities—into a visible expression of a new identity. The result as we know it: a strangely refracted representation of identity, viz. continuous movement outward implied in roads and fixedness implied in the identity of cities. To this is now added, of course, another tension by the contemporary growth of the mega-city, at once American/local as well as global/universal. What is better about such an identity? And for whom?

Conflicted Theory: City/Road/People

We might begin with the contexts of betterment. The heart of the ambiguity surrounding betterment lies, arguably, in the conflation of the symbolic meaning of the road/city. What is the relation between the hard, physical road of conquest and the "soft" road of cultural domination? It is clear that the cultural construction of America cannot be reduced to the ribbon of road, nor can the city be the sum of its buildings. One can glimpse the depth of the issue in Jonathan Raban's insightful book, *Soft City.* "The city as we imagine it, the soft city of illusion, myth, aspiration, and nightmare is as real, maybe more real than the hard city one can locate on maps, statistics, monographs on urban sociology, demography and architecture" (3).

Furthermore, the roads leading in and out of cities are rife with theoretical issues that, on inspection, mesh into the very problems facing cities. There is a notable similarity, if not a full-scale symmetry, between the two. While too complicated an issue to explore in full, a few suggestions might help us to see how the twentieth-century construction of roads and cities has opted for an alternative principle of betterment than that we witnessed above. The sense of religious and ethical betterment gives way to the appropriation of the public landscape for a nation-wide construction of a triumphant America whose relationship to the humble human is tentative at best. In effect, the American experience has been to continually shift the contexts of betterment.

In an original analysis released in 2002 as *The Seduction of Place: The City in the Twenty-First Century,* American architectural scholar Joseph Rykwert attempted to come to terms with the foundations of "place" in the modern city. It is, perhaps, not particularly surprising that he perceives discontent arising from the origin of the city itself. But strikingly, his ground-view analysis is rooted once again in the religious domain—a theme originating, as we saw above, with the Puritan founders. *The Seduction of Place* dwells, for example, on the dubious relationship of the city to deity, harkening to Genesis 4:17 wherein Cain, the villain of the story, builds a city, much to the displeasure of God, who would rather he had built a garden.

Rykwert's sketch of the beginnings of cities is so instructive that it deserves to be quoted in full. "So Scripture tells of the foundation of the first city by the first murderer in the land of Nod, the land of exile and vagabondage (that is what the name "Nod" means in Hebrew), as a shelter for humanity driven out of the garden of Eden. Many traditions—Chinese, Indian, African, European, Mesopotamian—speak of an analogous coming into settlement out of wandering, out of the nomadic condition. All these traditions reassert how dangerous that passage was, and insist that the beginning of every settlement had to be accompanied by rituals and sacrifices to placate the power of the place. Elaborate procedures were followed in accordance with divine creation, so that what was 'taken out of' nature physically and appropriated for human use could be restored to her as image and metaphor. Every city had its own gods, its own religion and calendar, and reckoned its own time from its foundation. In any given place time began when the city was founded" (13).

This ancient religious resistance to urban life and to the roads that bring access to it harbors conflicting human dimensions. In the example from Genesis, a mere journey to the city, even one for religious purposes, puts one not only in potential peril but, more importantly, out of sync with the will of divinity. Venturing into the city could even become an act of disobedience to God. Our culture has a handy term for this old notion of something being created with, by and for the gods—"the sacred." How does one keep in touch with the sacred? Foremost by traveling to it. If juxtaposed with the secular, there is indeed something sacred about familiar pathways turned into roads. No need to look further than the reverence bestowed on the esplanade leading to Lincoln's memorial. Not all roads are secular, either, including roads to a shrine. Some retain a kind of sacred purpose, even if only for the "public" and only on state occasions, as is the case with Philadelphia's famous parkway.

There is no hard and fast line between the sacred and the secular even in our culture, and the special sense of the road not only persists, but flares up in recent controversies. Communities regularly rise up in arms when new roads are to be pushed through for the benefit of "outsiders," many of whom don't respect what is perceived as the "sanctity" of the quiet, sedate homes in the previously undisturbed neighborhood. No differently, most good burghers of the suburbs will fight a superhighway being located anywhere near their "sacred" oasis of peace and quiet. What this means is that the notion of betterment argued on behalf of these new roads is a betterment largely defined by a sense of American grandeur or official "state" need, rather than by the moral and/or physical betterment of the community involved. Needless to say, when even such core notions as betterment become bitterly conflicted and contested, discontent blossoms throughout the country.

Roads, Cars and the Rational Construction of Social Space

The city, like the road, may be the locus of social and public space, but above all both are concrete, physical creations in need of concrete, physical space. Both lie, therefore, at the heart of the crisis precipitated by America's unchecked growth. This is so much so, in fact, that one is compelled to inquire into larger cultural questions looming behind this crisis. For instance, what factors shaped *urbs Americana* in its social/physical sense? Does Yankee capitalism have something to do with the problem?

Written in the 1960s, Henri Lefebvre's *The Urban Revolution* advances a point of view seldom encountered among urban theorists. Lefebvre, once a member of the French Communist Party (subsequently disavowed), saw both socialism and capitalism as ultimately cut from the same cloth. Both, he argued, were constituent elements essential to the understanding of the modern urban environment. Lefebvre contended that the urban world must be seen in the context of what preceded it: the agricultural city, followed by the mercantile one, which blended into the industrial mega-city. Standing on the threshold of the global metropolis, he urged theorists to look beyond the conflict between capitalism and socialism insofar as the current urban trends were making both irrelevant. He predicted, in fact, that urban development would develop any number of "blind fields," his phrase for ideologies that no longer reflected where the masses were moving. He envisioned the contemporary city as layered by political and social praxis, much of it out of sync with the wishes of most urban dwellers.

Most important, perhaps, was his view of city space, as one not to be conquered, limited, or imprisoned in any form. Space for the French theorist was the key intellectual means to grasp the new possibilities of social change. Influenced by Foucault's heterotopias, those centers of counterculture resident in all urban environments, Lefebvre regarded them as permanent spatial features of the metropolis. Consequently, in his mind, the modern city ought to change to reflect the diversity that was thundering into it. It had the potential to create a space and a spirit that would accommodate the multi-dimensional human of the future. It is sad, therefore, to compare his bold vision to the state of affairs today. Concern about human existence seems to be part of a larger contentious agenda … how can people even survive in the megalopolis? From Mumford's *The Culture of Cities* (1938) to Sommer's *Tight Places: Hard Architecture and How to Humanize It* (1974), the issue is what happens to the human element when up against urban pressures.

At the centre of the problem lies the conflict over that other creation of the American spirit, the automobile ... it has generated massive conflicts, not only in and of itself, but in what it has come to mean in the real and symbolic conquest of the North American environment. The car has become arguably the most dramatic tool in this conquest, and it has certainly profoundly changed the ways Americans relate to their country and to each other. *Yet, in an often overlooked dimension, it was not the car alone that laid waste, but the car and the city ... they worked in tandem.* Planting cities across the vast continent almost forced its conquest upon the nation-builders. Immense amounts of energy and intellectual effort, to say nothing of financing, were invested to bring the American vastness under control just to connect the citizens who moved from city to city, taking advantage of the roads that connected them. Movement was connected to city was connected to road. So thorough is this integration, in fact, that in *Space Replaces Us!* Michael Bell pleaded against the way in which the trio—movement, city, road—have conspired to remove the human dimension entirely from the equation.

In this kind of milieu, betterment has increasingly come to be defined by those who control the cultural priorities of public space. Oftentimes conflicts erupt over how the road is to define the city, or how city space is to be used for human, as opposed to "designer", purposes. In the 1980s the placing of *Tilted Arc* in New York's Federal Plaza became such a *cause celebre*. Richard Serra, a modernist sculptor, won a commission for a statue in the large round space in front of the Jacob K. Javits Federal Building. He fashioned a giant metal tilted arc that cut across the plaza, for all the world looking and acting, according to the critics, like a massive wall. The sculpture changed the whole orientation of the locals toward their space, and polarized the debate between the neo-conservatives and the liberals to such a degree that it touched off a national storm. The sense of the outrage was caught in a poem by a local attorney Donald Nawi:

> There was a plaza once.
> Now there is a steel wall.
> There was light there, air once.
> Now there is a steel wall.
> There were people once, mingling, looking, talking, sitting.
> Now there is a steel wall...
> There was something once.
> Now there is nothing.[16]

In the end, the clash between the hegemony of state and the public will was resolved. During the night of 15 March 1989, the federal government removed the giant sculpture and stored it in a Brooklyn warehouse. The case was important, however, because it demonstrated the rising tide of public opinion in the control of public city space. Local tastes came to have the upper hand in defining public spatial meaning. United against the idea that high-level planning and rationality dictate the make-up of a city, or that "designers" could measure the human dimension properly, an emergent cadre of writers and activists condemned the "rational" city and its attempt to overrule the locals. The conception of betterment has begun to shift away from grand schemes hatched at the national level.

Other conflicts precipitated genuinely protracted struggles… the classic case: Manhattan. Led by Robert Moses, the city had slated Washington Square for demolition in order to route an expressway through the area. Local citizens rebelled. The description of the battle, in a famous book by Jane Jacobs, *The Death and Life of Great American Cities* (1961), shows how ordinary people can exert pressure on city government to affirm the primacy of the community in defining how city space is used … standing against the demands of the car and the road. The Washington Square case affirms that city space is not owned by city government, but by the inhabitants. Cars do not trump people. Even in the context of the American conquest of physical space, the control of betterment has local boundaries.

Still, can betterment have any meaning at all within an environment in which the mere size of the city envelops and dwarfs the human being? Can it guarantee safety for various groups to navigate the city in which they live in separate boroughs, divorced from social intercourse with each other—except for street life? Is such a segmented city a place of betterment for its people? Not everyone sees modern urban models as conducive to the good life for the ordinary citizen. Writing contemporarily with Lefebvre, Georges Bataille expressed it in these memorable words:

> There is no truth when people look at each other as if they're separate individuals. Truth starts with shared conversations, shared laughter, friendship and it only happens going from one person to another. I hate the thought of a person being connected to isolation. The recluse who has the impression he reflects the world is ridiculous to my mind. He can't reflect it because, being himself a center of the reflection, he stops being able to relate to what doesn't have a center. As I picture it, the world doesn't resemble a separate or circumscribed being but what goes from one person to another when we laugh or make love. When I think this is the way things are, immensity opens and I'm lost. (44–5)

Since then, many other theorists and writers have joined in. Italo Calvino argued, for example, that "cities believe themselves to be the work either of the mind or of chance, but neither the first nor the second suffices to maintain their walls" (50). Thus, even though Lefebvre himself identifies the many influences that can shape the city's ideological and social complexity, even he seems to rely too much on the top-down rational model of urban life. In *The Imaginative Structure of the City* (2003), Alan Blum imagines the city in dramatically different terms: as an imaginative structure, full of anomalies and dissonance, much like a series of conversations.[17] It would appear that the penchant for strict (most often top-down) order among the rationalists and theorists of the city makes it difficult to accommodate what is really appealing about the city. By the same token, the pulse of the city is more sensitively and more cogently handled in works of literature.

Writers tap into that whole ... the "spirit" of the city, and the result is about as far from the New Jerusalem as one can imagine.

For some writers, the American city is the entrance to oblivion. Consider the case as stated by detective Quinn in Paul Auster's *City of Glass*. Published originally in 1985, it has been reissued since as part of the writer's *New York Trilogy:*

> New York was an inexhaustible space, a labyrinth of endless steps, and no matter how far he walked, no matter how well he came to know its neighborhoods and streets, it always left him with the feeling of being lost. Lost, not only in the city, but within himself as well. Each time he took a walk, he felt as though he were leaving himself behind, and by giving himself up to the movement of the streets, by reducing himself to a seeing eye, he was able to escape the obligation to think, and this, more than anything else, brought him a measure of peace, a salutary emptiness within. (4)

What a strange symmetry between the wasteland of the human soul and the heart of the American city. How had it come to this? Where is betterment when logic has gone and the road towards it has shifted from the Daughters of Zion to Hell's Angels?

Motoring into Crisis:
Road Triumph, Street Anguish, and the New Romantic Road

The Biblical negativity toward the city may have been bequeathed to American literature through its New England forbearers, but modern writers did not need help to identify sources of discontent with that other arm of betterment—the road. The early American roads had been poor physically, but not evil. A transformation occurred when writers began to follow Mrs. Knight in creating an American version of a European literary trope, creating the "bad" American road and the "bad" city street, indirectly feeding into the image of the "bad" city. Imbued with this negative symbolic meaning, streets and roads turned sinister, menacing, terror-ridden. Where the road in the colonial period was an adjunct of the city, a physical institution in liege to the goals of the millennium and the vehicle of the developing business, now it became a metaphor of a culture. The utilitarian road was transmuted into the Road.

Already by the early years in the twentieth century, a deep strand of the nation's identity has become rooted in the road. In 1923 Hilaire Belloc identified and discussed it at length in *The Road:*

> Not only is the Road one of the great human institutions because it is fundamental to social existence, but also because its varied effect appears in every department of the State. It is the Road which determines the sites of many cities and the growth and nourishment of all. It is the Road which gives its frame-work to all economic development. It is the Road which is the

channel of all trade and, what is more important, of all ideas. In its most humble function it is a necessary Guide without which progress from place to place would be a ceaseless experiment; it is a sustenance without which organized society would be impossible; thus ... the Road moves and controls all history (10).

Here some of the spirit of the City is appropriated for the Road.

The same ideas take shape in American writers of the era. In *A Traveler at Forty* (1913) and later *A Hoosier Holiday* (1916), the road takes Theodore Dreiser away from the gloom and disfiguration of the industrial city, a place (paradoxically) about whose brawn and commercial energy he waxed eloquent in other contexts. In a telling contrast, he revels in the joys and simple pleasures of America's countryside ... tiny picturesque villages and towns that he loved. There is high irony in this—a great writer whose road, city, country are being transformed into something else even as describes them. Even as journeying becomes a way of grasping who one really is, looking for the soul of "My America" must now take the writer off the beaten track. The "real" (in reality, romanticized) America now transcends its crippling industrial big-cities, and finds expression in the "fine-folk" towns of the country's interior. For Dreiser, the road was a memory lane taking him into the very heart of old-time America.

By the time John Steinbeck wrote *The Grapes of Wrath* (1939), of course, the road was indelibly linked to the American Dream gone bad. His Jim Casy, one-time preacher hounded by Granma to say a grace before the family head out on the road to California, could only wrestle with loss and discontent:

> I been in the hills, thinkin', almost you might say like Jesus went into the wilderness to think His way out of a mess of troubles ... I got thinkin' how we was holy when we was one thing, an' mankin' was holy when it was one thing. An' it on'y got unholy when one mis'able little fella got the bit in his teeth an' run off his own way, kickin' an' draggin' an' fightin'. Fella like that bust the holiness. But when they're all workin' together, not one fella for another fella, but one fella kind of harnessed to the whole shebang—that's right, that's holy. An' then I got thinkin' I don't even know what I mean by holy. (87–88)

This remarkable piece is enunciated on the eve of the Joads' epic trip into the "wilderness" of California, where they find no work but good American fellas who do everything to destroy them. The dream of an America pulled together by roads, of triumphant Zions connected by pleasant pathways, the same roads that were to lead to national betterment, evaporates with this Steinbeck classic which, together with *Of Mice and Men* and later on *Travels with Charley*, earned him the 1962 Nobel Prize in Literature. For this writer at least, the colonial experience and its dreams of betterment were all but dead.

What had changed from the old noble desire to tame the wildness with linking roads? At one level at least, we know that roads become linked directly to the movement and energy of the American dream. Since road-building was grounded in the nation's manifest destiny, an intellectual tradition blossomed that regarded such civic activities as highway construction as part of America's "civil religion." By the mid-twentieth century such activities have come to be regarded as important indicators of righteous betterment. After the Second War World, this principle was enshrined in concrete and asphalt by Lucius D. Clay—president of General Motors and Dwight Eisenhower's right-hand man on transportation—who wanted Americans to think in grand, continental terms. It was he who rallied the nation to pay trillions of dollars for the interstate system and to accept the challenge of the final conquest of American space. The move set up a society that was to enjoy the benefits of new linkages, and a street and road culture that grew up around them.

Historically, it is therefore hardly surprising that many postwar Americans began to look to travel as the symbolic expression of identity. The road and the car as cultural icons became the twin engines of transformation in this phase of American society. Somehow the city needed the highway to be free, to be American ...

Road Triumph, Street Anguish

Prevailing imagery of the road has always drawn from (and continues to be sustained by) popular culture, whether lowbrow or otherwise. From Valentine's Day news reports of the Capone-gang massacre on Chicago's Clark Street in 1929, to *Hate, Violence and Death on Main Street USA—A Report on Hate Crimes and Violence against People Experiencing Homelessness* in 2005, Americans are regularly exposed to the other side of the American Bad City streets.[18] In popular theater and cinema, a brilliant exponent of this theme was born when Arthur Laurents and Stephen Sondheim teamed up to write the book and lyrics for one of the greatest musicals of all time, *West Side Story* (1957). Symbolically, the dividing line between the turf of the Jets and the Sharks runs under a highway ... once again the road divides as surely as it provides the means to leave ethnic divisions—and everything else—behind. This is, after all, where Tony's life finally ebbs away, and where Maria is left to mourn a lost love and a destroyed future.

The roaring success of *West Side Story*, which combined the grimness of *noir* with the athletism of a Gene Kelly dance number, unleashed an avalanche of grim city streets into the mainstream in the 1960s. The same theme is evident wherever we look in the literature of this period. Piri Thomas's classic *Down the Mean Streets* (1967), whose title pays homage to Chandler and the hardboiled tradition, is all about boys growing into manhood in Spanish Harlem filled with violence on the "mean streets" of poverty and crime. S. E. Hinton's *Rumble Fish* (1975), whose Puerto Rican Fonzy is condemned by the very area in which he lives, finds the streets themselves indifferent to his fate.

Any lingering idea of betterment is characterized as slipping away from those who would seek it. Outside the city limits, Charles Eastman's *Little Fauss and Big Halsey* (1969) endlessly follows the pair of wandering motorcyclists down the road, looking for the big payoff that never comes. In the city, there is James Baldwin's *If Beale Street Could Talk* (1974), with its elegant portrayal of Harlem's ghetto ... the dead-end streets from which America's Blacks will never emerge. Some kind of climactic point is, finally, reached in the white-hot roads of drugs and counter-culture idolization of Hunter Thompson's *Fear and Loathing in Las Vegas* (1976). More than a decade of writing excursions into the heart of America's roads and city streets brings home a virulent criticism of the metaphysical highway America is on. It brings a mirror to the country's tattered soul that the betterment in the Puritan covenant was supposed to set right; it rankles even more in the face of what America has produced ... grim cities, grim roads.

Still, the loyalty to the "righteous" betterment of old continues to impact writing, even as the light it refracts on America becomes increasingly complex.[19] For example, millennial shadows of a moral kind can be found not only in William H. Whyte's *The Last Landscape* (1968), but in the work of his confréres, Christopher Tunnard and Boris Pushkarev, whose 1963 *Man-Made America—Chaos or Control*, won the National Book Award (and has been on architects' reading list ever since). The pair argued that America was heading into chaos unless it ushered in a careful kind of planning of urban space. Despite the growing antagonism to "designing" space in America, their argument is couched again in terms of betterment, this time aesthetic in nature. "A lake, a river, a factory, or a skyscraper," we read, "must all be set back from the freeway a sufficient distance for respect" (250). Needless to say, the American notion of betterment has always had trouble with this kind of "respect." The penchant for unobstructed development, loyalty to free enterprise, embrace of the car above rapid transit—these and other contentious policies simmer beneath the surface and constitute a continuing threat to the natural and aesthetic environment in the American collective ... what kind of respect is it that paves over America's beauty?

It is no surprise then that, beginning roughly with the 1980s, writing about roads and what they do becomes a catalyst for moral outrage—at times even a condemnation over what is driving American culture. Witness the brilliant quasi-apocalyptic critiques of Howard Kunstler, who castigates the shallowness of American urban life in *The Geography of Nowhere* (1992), and uses almost apocalyptic language in decrying the nation's thirst for oil in *The Long Emergency* (2005). The same restless sense of malaise is present in Jay McInerney's *Bright Lights, Big City*. His editor emeritus, Alex, "tells you there was the golden age of Papa and Fitzgerald and Faulkner, then a silver age in which he played a modest role. He thinks we're now in a bronze age, and that fiction has nowhere to go. It can run but it can't hide" (65). For McInerney things could not be more transparent: at the heart of the American dream lies decay.

In fact, the theme was already present in Thomas Pynchon's *V.* There, through chatter in the Belle Époque café, we learn the depth of America's decadence. "A decadence ... is a falling-away from what is human, and the farther we fall the less human we become. Because we are less human, we foist off the humanity we have lost on inanimate objects and abstract theories" (405). His is a telling criticism of the United States and its fixation on the then icon of technology, the car (now rapidly replaced by computers and telecommunications). Roads have by now morphed into a type of slickness—alien environmental and landscape forms built for special-interest groups, part of an American world bent in a direction antagonistic to the majority of plain folks. Pynchon sees this fixation as the later-day product of "sons" of Christianity and the American Dream, but whatever their version, the betterment contributed by religion to America is now plainly in eclipse.[20]

The principle theme in this period of American writing is that the positive dimensions of the American spirit have mutated on the country's road to destiny. Despite the expansive (and expensive!) dream of the Dwight Eisenhowers and Lucius Clays, among American writers road-building means more than the dollars-and-cents cost of asphalt and labor. It's a kind of mania of growth. Who says when enough is enough? As J. H. Kay shows in *Asphalt Nation: How the Automobile Took over America and How We Can Take It Back* (1997), it was expressed in the agony of passing miles of lifeless parking lots while trying to get out of town—there is an agony accompanying the non-stop expansion of the city. If one senses an outrage over how far America has strayed from its roots, it really is not new: forty years prior the Beat Generation had brought a deadening of soul into focus.

Via Dolorosa: From the Beats to Hell's Angels

It is a measure of how much America has drifted away from Nature itself that, beyond the mid-point of the twentieth century cities are not synonymous with freedom. Rather riding the roads became the symbol of freedom and real "nature." As the rockers Steppenwolf sang in a 1968 anthem, the space found on the road returns one to the true wild:

> Get your motor runnin' / Head out on the highway
> Lookin' for adventure / and whatever comes along ...
> Like a true nature's child / we were born to be wild
> We can climb so high / I never wanna die.

Madame Knight could never have comprehended such language being applied to the road, but the wildness now associated with the road certainly follows in her literary footsteps. Indeed, at some point the very notion of the road became a release from the American suburban homogeneity. From "Route 66" to "Goin' Down the Road" to the current Internet roadgeeks, cultural fads have attributed a transcending value to the humble road. Even as more and more Americans move to mega-city conurbations, with their nightmarishly snarled traffic and a pedestrian-unfriendly milieus, the old model of "road is space is freedom" still exerts considerable power.

The quintessential writer of this road power was Jack Kerouac. It was he who took the Beat Generation and gave it a full-bodied character. While mainstream America specialized in Cold War rhetoric, rattled nuclear armaments, and conscripted youngsters, he and Allen Ginsberg gave voice to a manifest and bitter dissent. Kerouac's novels became a kind of scripture for the Beats, and for countless readers since. In fact, if you believe Donald Miller, *On the Road* "had a greater impact on its readers than any other work of fiction in the 20th century." Writing about the road, Kerouac wrote about Neal Cassady, roadmaster and antithesis of the establishment: handsome, sensual, bisexual, compassionate, conman and "cocksman and Adonis of Denver" (14), as Ginsberg put it in 1956. Appearing in *On the Road* as Dean Moriarty, Cassady is described in curiously religious terms as a "new American saint" (194) who, Kerouac claims, brought him into touch with the new religion of IT—a kind of American version of the Eternal Now of Zen Buddhism.

In *The Daybreak Boys: Essays on the Literature of the Beat Generation* (1990), Gregory Stephenson goes as far as to attribute the fulcrum of the Beat movement to Cassady. "He is a catalyst—initiating, inciting action, urging others on to pleasure and abandon ... He is a prophet of the libido, of the instincts and appetites. His desperate hedonism is not, however, an end in itself but rather the means to an end: the transcendence of personal consciousness and time. His message, incoherent and inarticulately expressed, is of the perfection and essential unity of all experience" (10). A decade later, in the midst of another counterculture revolution that swept America, Tom Wolfe wrote of Cassady in *The Kandy-kolored Tangerine-flake Streamline Baby* (1965) and placed him front and center in *The Electric Kool-Aid Acid Test* (1968). As the literary collector and historian of the period, Donald Miller, points out in *Books by the Beat Generation* (2004), Wolfe, too, deferred to the living legend of Cassady, depicting him as a mythic figure in pursuit of "the westernmost edge of experience."

Even if the road that Cassady, Kerouac and Ginsberg journeyed on was a lonely one, the theme of prophetic mission prevails in their writings. Here was betterment played in a different tune. The travelers see themselves as leading a New Wave or propounding a New Era, as another Beat writer, Diane DiPrima, described it in 1969. Indeed, their literature transformed the American journey into an existential exploration, and hitting the road into a quasi-religious transformative experience. Offering a clear alternative to the stifling middle class and their boring cities, in the 1960s the road trip took on a new meaning. With Ken Kesey's group of Merry Pranksters (including the ubiquitous Neal Cassady), whose psychedelic bus roamed across America with no destination in mind other than to experience the Eternal Now, a new transcendence developed. In turn, another generation of American writers became energized by their experience. Some, like Robert Pirsig in his 1974 smash bestseller *Zen and the Art of Motorcycle Maintenance*, connected it to Eastern religions, paving the way for the Buddhist enlightenment to enter popular consciousness and the spreading New Age subculture. Religious betterment was at work again, but in a strange new formulation ... from a strange Eastern religious clime.

And then there was the motorcycle. For some like Pirsig, the motorbike was the ultimate machine for encountering the inner truth of things. For others, as in Arlo Guthrie's "Motorcycle Song," it was a medium for good-natured social critique. For others still, it took on sinister dimensions. It could be the open door to absolute dissent, a type of Anti-Christ. That was the image cultivated by the Hell's Angels, bane of enforcement agencies, a new kind of mafia, radical evil on the roads. The organization cultivated its sinister, devil-inspired subculture, importing into its paraphernalia religious symbols, like the famous "mark of the beast" from the Book of Revelations in the New Testament (though, needless to say, employed at cross-purposes with the original). Thus we hear from Hell's Angels writer, Frank Reynolds: "The sign 666 to me means, in my own words, a follower in the sense of Hell's Angels. Nearer to Satan than the average normal human being can be. I feel as though I am part of him" (127).

Hearing this, for many Americans, the neutral (not to say the benign) nature of the road in connecting states, cities and communities seemed to have evaporated completely. Now the roads could be used by criminals to hit and run at cities and people. Inconceivably roads were part of a system that had to be challenged for the greater public good of America. The very sources of early America's betterment seem to have disappeared, and the counterculture has taken over its main symbols. The Road has become a *via dolorosa*.

The Road to New Romance and Personality

Even if the trajectory that had begun with Sarah Kemble Knight had come to an end in chaos, the existence of the road out of the city across the continent bred new possibilities. It was the key to a much more sophisticated religio-philosophical purchase on the American spirit ... for, once the trip itself becomes an end in itself, one can embark on a *quest*. One no longer seeks the magic of the city ... it is the adventure, the sights and sounds of the road that become meaningful goals in themselves. As expressed in Mark K. (Tiger) Edmonds's poetry, partly reproduced in his online essay, "Literature of the American Road":

> My Grandfather used to say to me,
> Boy tell me where it was you went to.
> Tell me about the things you've seen.
> He'd want to know all about the sights
>   and the names and the places
>   and about my highway machine.

In 1988, armed with a cassette-tapeful of poems called *Gather 'Round Me, Riders*, Tiger Edmonds set out on the road to extol the virtues of free travel. Eventually he brought his poems out in *Longrider: A Tale of Just Passin' Through* (1998), which propelled his writing into the mainstream. Alongside Peter S. Beagle's *I See by My Outfit* (1965), Thompson's insightful *Fear and Loathing in Las Vegas* (1976), William Least Heat Moon's *Blue Highways: A Journey into America* (1982), the renaissance in American Roadlit was well on its way. More recently there would come Robert Kaplan's *An Empire Wilderness: Travels into America's Future* (1998) and Larry McMurty's *Roads: Driving America's Great Highways* (2001), both extolling an almost religious vision of America's greatness, accessible to those who would journey to experience it from up close. Where is the city here? The contrast with Chandleresque mean city streets could not be greater, showing how dramatic the change has been.

From the perspective of recent American literature, you might just as well escape the Big Bad City ... plagued by bad power structures and bad policies ... best to hit the road and discover an America unsullied by the evils of the mega-urban society. True, the road no longer connects you directly to a pristine countryside or a distinctively crafted little town, but it still provides a chance to meet the colorful characters of America's spirited road life. *The Road delivers real people to you, something the big city can't do.* In Gabel and Hahn's *Anthem: An American Road Story*, the road offers a chance to visit some of the great personalities of a road trip ... Hunter Thompson of Beat fame, George McGovern and George Stephanopoulos of political fame, Willie Nelson of music, and others. Here is another transition: the road is less a linkage than the means to encounter America's diverse characters—its individual souls. Tellingly, the book's frontispiece even quotes from Steinbeck's *Travels with Charley: In Search of America*: "A journey is a person in itself; no two are alike. And all plans, safeguards, policing, and coercion are fruitless. We find after years of struggle that we do not take a trip; a trip takes us."

The road has become the way to self-fulfillment and personal discovery. Freed from the ills of the city, the true American spirit can be won in the exquisite movement of journeying to genuine people. In *Longrider*, Tiger Edmonds connects roads to the past, as vehicles of memory:

> The highway calls and the distance beckons.
> I chase ancient memories,
> pursue primeval passions.
> It's gypsy nomad wanderlust,
>   all in a scooter- trash fashion. (3)

How are we to understand this new, rather sophisticated view of the American situation? If one steps back and views the panorama of literature from Mark Twain through Kerouac to McMurtry, we can see how the urban environment increasingly oriented the road for the city's benefit. In this new, somewhat surprising take on betterment, however, the Road becomes a vehicle for personal encounters with a still great America, its characters. This embrace of genuine American continentalism, mediated by the car and lots of roads to conquer the land with, but focusing on people is caught in Ronald Primeau's *The Romance of the Road: The Literature of the American Highway* (1996). Space and road are perceived in terms other than the old dichotomies. Set aside is the establishment roads for purposes of conquest; so is the anti-establishment rejection thereof by the Beats or Hell's Angels. We encounter the representation of the real personality of America, removed from the urban slickness and/or blight of the city, in a trope of discovery and romance not seen since the early days.

Gone, now, is Kemble Knight's rugged road to Boston, gone is the City of God, gone the New Jerusalem, gone the grandeur of vision. Instead, present-day American writing unveils a wealth of little dramas, staged on roads that have no meaning other than means for getting you there. The road retreats into a cultural fixture of finding the American spirit, as if that spirit had somehow hidden itself in the very movement from one place to another. The city is a lost space, good for selling books out of the backs of cars—as did Terri Woods in August 2005, taking back Harlem street life by so doing—but seriously delinquent in symbolizing the best of the American spirit. Indeed, it is almost as if true Nature is now to be found in the character of Americans themselves. But what becomes of betterment?

Writers' Denouement

Two historical themes emerge from our exploration of American writers and American experience, both of which have been influenced by the sense of betterment. First, is the transformation of the principal symbols of American achievement: the City and the Road into mixed secular/religious idioms. The millennial sentiment of social and religious improvement, articulated early on in myriad ways by America's writers, has increasingly moved beyond a purely religious arena into the political—to be ultimately enshrined in America's cultural consciousness through Martin Luther King's unforgettable "I have a Dream" address in front of Lincoln's memorial. In this way betterment now has a larger purchase on the American articulation of its culture of democracy.

Where cities and roads were initially attached to a social and moral betterment, they themselves are increasingly divorced from it, even turning diabolical. In literature, they take on a sinister character in and of themselves. Faced with the reality of America's streets and roads in the alien mega-city, literary representation has moved towards a vision of the city's culture immersed in a kind of madness, with the very road as part of a larger agenda—a conspiracy if you will—that one must face in today's world just to survive.

The second historical trend is loss of a unifying destiny. Locally generated values infuse social meaning with personal goals, sometimes of a religious sort, sometimes of a business sort, sometimes of a non-rational sort, allowing for a multi-dimensional critique of society, while encouraging the private experience as a basis for measuring the success of American culture. Strangely, this trend to incorporate intensely personal perceptions of betterment into America's distinctive goals, while allowing generation after generation to re-interpret their relationship to America with perspectives arising out of their time, place and spirit, at the same time contributes to a lessening of the corporate vision. In this literary individualizing of America, the romantic roads of today's writers are a telling reflection of the decay of a corporate manifest destiny.

Still, it must be acknowledged that the trend to personalizing road/city culture is not completely new, for there are echoes within America's literature at recurring moments. There it is part of both a sense of identity and continuing conflict. What it does do at this moment is to blur the distinctiveness of the American city precisely at a moment when international enterprise moves to modeling an international mega-city. The result is that the conceptions of the city/road we have explored here reflect primarily the critical shift among American writers of the genre away from a geographic to a cultural idiom. The result frees the American city/road from its locale. Thus, the writer articulates a kind of denouement: the decaying American city is enshrined in literature precisely as that city becomes the image of the global mega-city—and that without the refined constraint of betterment.

CHAPTER 5

Urbs Americana:

A WORK IN PROGRESS

William John Kyle

In the opening sentence of the first chapter of *The Age of Reform*, the American historian Richard Hofstadter aptly remarked that "the United States was born in the country and has moved to the city" (23). In fact, few nations have urbanized more rapidly and more extensively. Urbanization is by definition a process whereby the number of urban dwellers increases in relation to rural dwellers. At the time of the signing of the Constitution, American society was overwhelmingly rural (95 percent) and agricultural. Over the course of the nineteenth century the United States developed a vast network of cities, so that by 1920 its urban population exceeded that of the rural areas. This process unfolded throughout the twentieth century and continues unabated today. American urbanization has involved changes in form and social character that help to illuminate broader changes in the nation's social and economic evolution, and which provide insight into that continuing work in progress—*Urbs Americana.*

On a broad historical scale, the development of American cities has been divided into distinct phases based on prevailing transportation technology and the major sources of industrial energy. Each of these five epochs—prior to 1830, from 1830 to 1870, from 1870 to 1920, from 1920 to 1970, and post-1970—is also readily associated with significant features of settlement, economy, and technological change in the nation (Borchert, 1967). The first of them, termed by Borchert the *Sail-Wagon Epoch*, ended around 1830 and was marked by generally primitive modes of overland and waterway circulation. In colonial days, settlements were mainly oriented towards the sea, so that the leading cities were the northeastern ports that were heavily oriented to European overseas trade rather than to their, at that time, barely accessible hinterlands. They drew their form and structure on the walking scale: compact pedestrian-oriented settlements in which everything needed for daily life was available within a 30-minute stroll.

Much of the 19th-century history of the United States, and particularly the first seven decades, is intimately associated with the westward movement of people across the continent. This continental expansion and the progress of American urbanization were mutually reinforcing in a myriad of ways. Changes in the economy, the evolving development of a national market, and a succession of developments in communication and transportation that took place during this time further stimulated unprecedented urban growth. In fact, the arrival and spread of the steam-powered railroad heralded Borchert's second era, the *Iron Horse Epoch*, which lasted for about forty years from 1830 to 1870. During that time a nationwide transport system was forged steadily and a national urban system began to take shape, with New York City emerging by 1850 as the prime city in the nation.

The third era, the *Steel-Rail Epoch*, spanned the decades of the Industrial Revolution. The forces shaping the economic, and thus urban, growth during this time were the increasing scale of manufacturing, the rise of the steel and automobile industries in the Midwest, and the introduction of steel rails that enabled significant advances in the speed and carrying capacity of the railroads (the dominant mode of transport throughout this era). By the close of this period, a national urban system had become fully established. Encompassing the years from 1870 to 1920, it can be viewed as a period of maturation of the American urban system, where the previous one had been more formative in its basic characteristics. The existing big cities became bigger, even as a rapid population increase, massive immigration from rural areas and from overseas, and burgeoning economic growth led to a multiplication of city functions.

Manufacturing was usually at the core of this phenomenal growth. Concurrently, the development of technology, which facilitated movement of people both vertically (elevators) and horizontally (electric-powered streetcars), provided a stimulus for a dramatic reorganization of the urban form. Tall central-city office buildings and business blocks began to agglomerate in a central business district (or CBD), which took on a striking new appearance and a new command-and-control function. While the central city soared further upward, the urban areas also expanded outward, producing the now familiar pattern of core CBD, inner-city slums and blue-collar areas, and a ring of generally more affluent suburbs. Changes in the physical form were accompanied by changes in the social composition of American cities. One way or another, by the end of this tumultuous period of urban development the nation's basic urban system was firmly established.

By 1920, half of the nation's population was living in urban centers, and their proportion continued to grow throughout the century, reaching four-fifths today. The period from 1920 to 1970, termed the *Auto-Air-Amenity Epoch*, is characterized by the following key elements: the automobile and the airplane, the expansion of white-collar service employment, and the growing pull of amenities, or pleasant environments, that increasingly stimulated urbanization of the suburbs and selected regional locales. It was a period in which the automobile and later the airplane shaped newer cities and reshaped older ones, encouraging—particularly from the 1950s onwards—a new kind of decentralization. The process undermined the power and status of the central city, which lost political and social importance in relation to the sprawling subcenters within an ever-expanding urban region. This period can also be said to encompass the last stage of industrial urbanization and the maturation of the national urban hierarchy.

The final stage, the *Satellite-Electronic-Jet Propulsion Epoch*, is currently being shaped by advances in information management, computer technologies, global communications and intercontinental travel. As such, it tends to favor globally oriented metropolises, particularly those along the Pacific and Atlantic coasts, that function as international gateways. Since 1970 significant changes in urban population trends have heralded a new period of urban development characterized by periods of expansion and counter-urbanization, both of which take place against a background of massive megalopolitan agglomerations across the country.

The Evolution and Expansion of the American Urban System

In the early colonial period, prior to about 1800, small communities began to emerge along the Atlantic seaboard, mostly in what are now New England and the Middle Atlantic states. Their development was a natural outcome of being situated nearest to the European colonial nations which were the source of people, capital and consumer goods. As a result, merchandising establishments were more advantageously located in port towns from which goods could be readily distributed, even as settlement expanded into the interior. Those same settlements were also the favored locations for assembling and exporting raw materials back to Europe as well as for performing what little processing was needed for shipment abroad.

From the initially great number of small ports, four in particular—Baltimore, Boston, New York City, and Philadelphia—soon began to dominate the urban hierarchy. In the colonial South, although both Charleston (South Carolina) and Savannah (Georgia) were founded early and developed diverse port and urban functions, the self-sufficiency of the plantation economy was in the main inimical to the development of towns. Not surprisingly, in a relatively short time it became clear that neither would seriously rival the North in terms of urban development. All the same, at the time of the first 1790 census of the newly formed United States (Table 5.1), there were no communities with over 50,000 inhabitants. Only five—New York, Philadelphia, Boston, Charleston, and Baltimore—had more than 10,000, and of these only Charleston was in the colonial South. Primarily oriented towards the European trade, each port served a small local hinterland, none showing any indication of urban dominance at that time.

Table 5.1 Population of the Twenty-four Urban Places in the United States: 1790

Rank	Place	Population
1	New York City, NY	33,131
2	Philadelphia City, PA	28,522
3	Boston Town, MA	18,320
4	Charleston City, SC	16,359
5	Baltimore Town, MD	13,503
6	Northern Liberties Township, PA	9,913
7	Salem Town, MA	7,921
8	Newport Town, RI	6,716
9	Providence Town, RI	6,380
10=	Marblehead Town, MA	5,661
10=	Southwark District, PA	5,661
12	Gloucester Town, MA	5,317
13	Newburyport Town, MA	4,837
14	Portsmouth Town, NH	4,720
15	Sherburne Town (Nantucket), MA	4,620
16	Middleborough Town, MA	4,526
17	New Haven City, CT	4,487
18	Richmond City, VA	3,761
19	Albany City, NY	3,498
20	Norfolk Borough, VA	2,959
21	Petersburg Town, VA	2,828
22	Alexandria Town, VA	2,748
23	Hartford City, CT	2,683
24	Hudson City, NY	2,584

Source: *US Bureau of the Census*
Internet Release date: June 15, 1998

The period from 1800 to 1870 encompasses the era of the great push westward and the opening up of the American continent for settlement. Early on the use of inland waterways, such as the Ohio River, the lower Great Lakes, and the Erie Canal led to the establishment of inland urban centers such as Richmond (Virginia), Lancaster and Pittsburgh (Pennsylvania), and Albany (New York). Later they were joined by St. Louis (Missouri), Cincinnati (Ohio), and Louisville (Kentucky), as well as Buffalo and Rochester (New York). Nevertheless, the Atlantic ports retained their regional supremacy, and with the Louisiana Purchase in 1803, another primary Atlantic port, New Orleans, was added to the national inventory.

Despite the growth of manufacturing, usually oriented towards households and small workshops, rural and agricultural activity still dominated until around the 1840s. Thereafter the establishment of the factory system and the development of the railways galvanized the industrial functions more closely associated with urban centers. The large port cities grew in size and in importance with the construction of canals, roads and railways to the interior. A series of regional rail networks developed, with the larger networks converging at important inland waterway connections. As a consequence, each prominent coastal port began to organize its own railway system and push it inland to tap the interior for its own economic benefit.

Before the middle of the century, industrialization was subordinate to basic production, except in the big Atlantic port cities that dominated trade relationships between the agricultural economy of North America and Europe. The mercantile ethos continued to be pervasive in most other cities for some time, although gradually industrial development and urban growth became more closely intertwined. The supply of manufacturing labor was enhanced by the attraction of farm youths to cities and by accelerating immigration from overseas, at this time mainly from Europe. After 1840 foreign immigrants began to concentrate on the edge of the expanding central business district in many urban areas, presaging the large-scale development of the ethnic ghettos.

It was at this time that New York City sprinted to undisputed continental primacy. The city owed it partly to the opening of the Erie Canal which cemented its western trade advantages over competitors, and because it was able to control much of the external trade of the South. As David Ward (1971) has pointed out, "It was largely because the merchants of New York and their itinerant factors controlled the cotton trade that urbanization in the South was extremely slow" (29). Consequently, neither Charleston nor New Orleans was able to wrest control of the cotton trade from the Big Apple. In the first fifty years of the nineteenth century, New York City grew from being roughly equal in size to Boston and Philadelphia (its nearest rivals) to a population that exceeded half a million, more than twice that of any other city on the continent.

Inland, urbanization was mostly limited to the Ohio River valley (Cincinnati, Pittsburgh, and Louisville) and upstate New York (Albany, Rochester, and Buffalo). From the 1860s onwards, however, urban populations began to explode throughout the newly opened Midwest. By 1870 no less than 168 cities had populations over 10,000, and 14 over 100,000. Water transport helped places like Cincinnati and St. Louis to grow rapidly, but by 1870 they were being challenged by the booming Great Lakes cities of Detroit, Milwaukee, Cleveland, and especially Chicago.

Brisk urban growth continued in New England and the Middle Atlantic states, particularly in the vicinity of New York City. Brooklyn ranked as the third largest city in the country, while both Newark and Jersey City (New Jersey) were in the top twenty. In the South, only New Orleans (with a population of almost 200,000) continued to grow, whereas in the West the only substantial city was San Francisco with nearly 150,000 people (Table 5.2). In short, urban development, particularly in the eastern half of the country, was revolutionized during this period by the development of an inter-regional transportation system combining rail networks with inland waterways. Although industrial growth was an important stimulant in the larger cities, it was only later that major industrial development came to play a role as an engine of urban growth.

Table 5.2 Population of the Twenty Largest Urban Places in the United States: 1870

Rank	Place	Population
1	New York City, NY	942,292
2	Philadelphia, PA	674,022
3	Brooklyn, NY	396,099
4	St. Louis, MO	310,864
5	Chicago, IL	298,977
6	Baltimore, MD	267,354
7	Boston, MA	250,526
8	Cincinnati, OH	216,329
9	New Orleans, LA	191,418
10	San Francisco, CA	149,473
11	Buffalo, NY	117,714
12	Washington, DC	109,199
13	Newark, NJ	105,059
14	Louisville, KY	100,753
15	Cleveland, OH	92,829
16	Pittsburgh, PA	86,076
17	Jersey City, NJ	82,546
18	Detroit, MI	79,577
19	Milwaukee, WI	71,440
20	Albany, NY	69,422

Source: *US Bureau of the Census*
Internet Release date: June 15, 1998

The period from 1870 to 1920 was one of maturation for the American urban system. On the one hand, national transportation systems were largely completed, and national accessibility was extended to the South, the Southwest, and eventually the Far West. The remaining agricultural lands of the West were opened for settlement, and a variety of rich mineral deposits were discovered and developed. Even as the economy gradually evolved from primarily commercial-mercantile to industrial-capitalistic in character, the chief stimulus to urban growth was industrial development.

Although coastal cities continued to thrive, much of the growth was concentrated in the Manufacturing Belt of the Northeast. After the Civil War, the geographical division of labor—a basis for present-day regionalism—was already becoming apparent. The decades that followed were ones of accelerated westward movement, rapid population increase, heavy immigration from overseas, and burgeoning urban growth. Although the functions of cities continued to multiply, at their core was usually the growth of manufacturing. Small towns sprouted where none had existed before with amazing rapidity, big towns grew into large cities, and the latter burgeoned into metropolises. While the rural population roughly doubled during this time, the urban population multiplied almost sevenfold. The biggest cities of the Midwest grew wildly, with Chicago more than doubling its population in the single decade 1880–90. Others like Detroit, Milwaukee, Columbus and Cleveland grew by a staggering 60 to 80 percent. Similar trends were observed in smaller centers. In California, Los Angeles experienced the early stages of what was to become a spectacular population explosion in the twentieth century, and there were boom times in places as diverse as Appalachian coal towns and the Carolina Piedmont.

Table 5.3   Population of the Twenty Largest Urban Places in the United States: 1920

Rank	Place	Population
1	New York City, NY	5,620,048
2	Chicago, IL	2,701,705
3	Philadelphia, PA	1,823,779
4	Detroit, MI	993,078
5	Cleveland, OH	796,841
6	St. Louis, MO	772,897
7	Boston, MA	748,060
8	Baltimore, MD	733,826
9	Pittsburgh, PA	588,343
10	Los Angeles, CA	576,673
11	Buffalo, NY	506,775
12	San Francisco, CA	506,676
13	Milwaukee, WI	457,147
14	Washington, DC	437,571
15	Newark, NJ	414,524
16	Cincinnati, OH	401,247
17	New Orleans, LA	387,219
18	Minneapolis, MN	380,582
19	Kansas City, MO	324,410
20	Seattle, WA	315,312

Source: *US Bureau of the Census*
Internet Release date: June 15, 1998

By 1920, after this chaotic period of expansion, the basic urban system of the country was firmly in place (Table 5.3). Half of the nation's population was urban, and this proportion continued to increase as the century progressed. Growth continued unabated in the older urban areas, but the most dramatic changes took place in newer cities, far removed from the traditional urban centers: the West Coast, Florida, Texas, the desert Southwest, and the eastern side of the Rockies. By the beginning of the 1960s, about 55 percent of the population lived in urban centers with populations greater than 25,000. Typical features included agglomeration, urban sprawl, freeway construction, central-city decay, urban renewal, urban air pollution, suburban high rises, concerted desegregation efforts, planned industrial districts, and extensive neighborhood and regional shopping centers.

The post-1920 period is set apart by the remarkable role played by the automobile (and later by air travel) in shaping newer cities and in reshaping older ones. The development of America's roads during the so-called "Century of the Automobile" has been extensively covered in William Kaszynski's *The American Highway: The History and Culture of Roads in the United States* (2000). At the turn of the last century, automobiles were showing promise as convenient and efficient transportation but were still considered a novelty available only to the city rich. In 1900 there were only about 8,000 cars in the nation, and outside of the cities roads were little more than glorified dirt tracks. Kaszynski considers the history of American roads to have taken place in four main phases: *The Early Days* from 1900 to 1919; *The First Generation* from 1920 to 1945; *The Golden Age* from 1946 to 1969; and *The Modern Interstate Era* from 1970 to the present.

A key characteristic of *The Early Days* was the steady increase in the production of automobiles, in no small measure the triumph of Henry Ford's Model T, affectionately known as "Tin Lizzie." The vehicle was nothing fancy but the body had a higher than normal clearance, a distinctive advantage given the poor state of roads at that time. Between 1908 and 1916 the number of cars in America exploded to nearly 2.5 million, bringing pressure to improve the road and highway systems. The decades between the World Wars—usually divided into the Roaring Twenties of gaiety and opulence, and the drab hard times of the Depression in the thirties—saw the American road network transformed from an incomplete collection of dirt and mud ribbons to a nationwide system of reliable, hard-surfaced highways. The automobile and this growing complex of all-weather roads provided Americans with an alternative, personalized means of travel which allowed more individual freedom and ushered in increased personal mobility that would have far-reaching consequences for the evolution of the urban system.

A key event during this era was the 1939 World's Fair in New York City, including the *Futurama* exhibit, sponsored by General Motors Corporation (Fox, 2004). The exhibition provided a tantalizing glimpse of the future for Americans emerging from the dark days of the Great Depression, one that involved big multi-lane superhighways on which cars would travel at 100 mph. On leaving the exhibit, visitors were given buttons which read I HAVE SEEN THE FUTURE, and certainly they had seen a part of it. Today such multiple multi-lane highways form part of the Eisenhower Interstate Highway System, built with federal funds between 1956 and 1993, and connecting American cities and people in a web of roads that some see as the lifeline of the nation.

But that is not the whole story. Although this greatest public works project ever "did lead to an America that is more mobile, less plagued by regional differences, and vastly wealthier than before, the construction changed the country in ways that could not be foreseen in 1939 or even in 1956" (Fox, 78). It enabled Americans to speed across the country and into vast stretches of wilderness, yet it distanced them from the very land they sought. It added new words to the national vocabulary, such as beltway or drive time, even as it provided new meanings for old ones, like smog, pollution, ecology, environment, traffic jam and pile up.

The Interstate System was intensely marketed as a savior both for the rural America and for the declining urban cores. The freeways afforded those who had once had to live in the city and walk to work at a factory a chance to have a home in the relative safety, privacy, quiet and cleanliness of the suburban countryside. In other words, it accelerated the trend towards suburbanization at the expense of both the city and the country. Not surprisingly, citing a Bureau of Labor Statistics survey for home building in the six largest metropolitan areas for 1946–47, Kenneth Jackson notes that over 62 percent of all home construction occurred in suburban areas (page 238). US Census data show that, during 1950–60, central-city populations in the largest twenty-five metropolitan areas increased by just over 3 percent, while the total suburban populations increased by well over 60 percent.

Beginning in the mid-1960s, however, many began to blame the unchecked growth of the highway system for a spate of social problems. Oftentimes city neighborhoods were chopped up and destroyed, and downtown areas abandoned for the easy access malls that mushroomed at Interstate exit ramps. Roads and highways made long-distance commuting feasible, and thereby were accused of contributing to the "white flight" that segregated races and social classes from one another. While the total populations of the largest cities stagnated, the number of blacks in the central cores increased greatly, indicating an urban *depopulation* by whites who migrated to the suburban fringes.

More often than not, the routeways were also laid down in the neighborhoods occupied predominantly by African-Americans, Hispanics and other minorities— people who did not possess the political clout to challenge construction. In the early years the burgeoning routeways seemed a shining example of social advance and visionary management, but by the 1970s they had helped sour many Americans to the very idea of progress and good government. In the ensuing years, planners and residents alike found that highways had the power to divide rather than unite, transforming once vibrant city neighborhoods into cold, alien cityscapes.

Table 5.4 Population of the Twenty Largest Urban Places in the United States: 1970

Rank	Place	Population
1	New York City, NY	7,894,862
2	Chicago, IL	3,366,957
3	Los Angeles, CA	2,816,061
4	Philadelphia, PA	1,948,609
5	Detroit, MI	1,511,482
6	Houston, TX	1,232,802
7	Baltimore, MD	905,759
8	Dallas, TX	844,401
9	Washington, DC	756,510
10	Cleveland, OH	750,903
11	Indianapolis, IN	744,624
12	Milwaukee, WI	717,099
13	San Francisco, CA	715,674
14	San Diego, CA	696,769
15	San Antonio, TX	654,153
16	Boston, MA	641,071
17	Memphis, TN	623,530
18	St. Louis, MO	622,236
19	New Orleans, LA	593,471
20	Phoenix, AZ	581,562

Source: *US Bureau of the Census*
Internet Release date: June 15, 1998

Although Borchert's (1967) fourth epoch ends in 1970 (Table 5.4), even as the *Satellite-Electronic-Jet Propulsion Epoch* begins, there is little doubt that the changes that took place over the last thirty-five years are ultimately rooted in the preceding era. Indeed, the data in Table 5.4 reveal a rather biased picture of the national urban system, inasmuch as the figures refer to the population of legally defined central cities and not to the reality of much bigger urban agglomerations. Since 1950 there have been major changes in the distribution of people, in the structure of the economy, in technology and living standards, and in the relative importance of different regions, cities and metropolitan areas.

Between 1950 and 2005 the country's population grew by 94 per cent, from 152 million to over 295 million. Over the same period, the proportion of people living in urban areas rose from 62 to 80 percent. Under these conditions, aided by the rapid diffusion of communications technologies and the lifestyle homogeneity produced by mass consumption, the traditional urban-rural dichotomy seems now to have lost any real meaning. The rate of economic growth has been even greater over the same period, despite a number of severe economic recessions. This growth in income, wealth and production has, in turn, provided the context for the continued redistribution of population and massive economic restructuring that has both underlain, and generated substantial changes in, the urban system (Mills and McDonald, 1994).

The central story of the last sixty-five years of urbanization has been the emergence of a country-wide system of metropolitan areas that dominate the nation economically and socially. The US Census Bureau first designated them in 1949 as "standard metropolitan area" or SMA. Ten years later the term was modified to "standard metropolitan statistical area" or SMSA. A further change in nomenclature occurred in 1983 with the introduction of the terms "metropolitan statistical area" or MSA, "consolidated metropolitan statistical area" or CMSA, and "primary metropolitan statistical area" or PMSA. The best known term, "metropolitan area" or MA, was adopted in 1990 and is used to refer collectively to MSAs, CMSAs and PMSAs (US Census Bureau, 1999).

In 1950 the US Census recorded 169 standard metropolitan areas comprising nearly 85 million people, or 56 percent of the national population. By 2000 there were no less than 261 MSAs and 19 CMSAs. Combined, these 280 metropolitan areas were home to some 208 million people, or almost 80 percent of all people living in America (US Census Bureau, 2001). In just five years since, this already colossal number of metropolitan areas had further risen to 369 (US Census Bureau, 2006). Furthermore, the degree of concentration of both population and economic activity is even higher than these figures suggest. From 1950 to 2000, for example, the number of metropolitan areas with a population of more than a million increased from fourteen to fifty, home to nearly 164 million people or almost 60 percent of the populace.

Some of these metropolises are now of such immense size that they cross several state boundaries. According to the 2000 census (US Census Bureau, 2001), the metropolitan area of New York–Northern New Jersey–Long Island has a combined population of more than 21 million, extending over four states (New York, New Jersey, Connecticut and Pennsylvania). The Los Angeles–Riverside–Orange CMSA houses more than 16 million people, and the Chicago–Gary–Kenosha CMSA (extending over Illinois, Indiana and Wisconsin) more than 9 million. Even the second-tier metropolitan areas are home to huge numbers of people, with Washington–Baltimore CMSA (7.6 million), and the San Francisco–Oakland–San Jose CMSA (7 million), occupying the remaining two places in the top five. Many of the newer metropolitan centers, such as Dallas–Fort Worth (5. 2 million), and Houston–Galveston–Brazonia (4.7 million), which occupy ninth and tenth places respectively, are also bursting in size and expanding rapidly. These ten largest metropolitan areas together account for almost one-third of the total US population (Table 5.5).

Table 5.5   Population (1,000s) of the Thirty-three Metropolitan Areas in the United States
with Populations over 1.5 million: 2000

Rank	Place	Pop. 2000	Pop. 1990	Percent change 1990 to 2000
1	New York City–North New Jersey–Long Island, NY/NJ/CT/PA	21,200	18,550	9.6
2	Los Angeles–Riverside–Orange, CA	16,374	14,532	12.7
3	Chicago–Gary–Kenosha, IL/IN/WI	9,158	8,240	11.1
4	Washington–Baltimore DC/MD/VA/WV	7,608	6,727	13.1
5	San Francisco–Oakland–San Jose, CA	7,039	6,253	12.6
6	Philadelphia–Wilmington–Atlantic City, PA/NJ/DE/MD	6,188	5,893	5.0
7	Boston–Worcester–Lawrence, MA/NH/ME/CT	5,819	5,455	6.7
8	Detroit–Ann Arbor–Flint, MI	5,456	5,187	5.2
9	Dallas–Ft.Worth, TX	5,222	4,037	29.3
10	Houston–Galveston–Brazonia, TX	4,670	3,731	25.2
11	Atlanta, GA	4,112	2,960	38.9
12	Miami–Ft.Lauderdale, FL	3,876	3,193	21.4
13	Seattle–Tacoma–Bremerton, WA	3,555	2,970	19.7
14	Phoenix–Mesa, AZ	3,252	2,238	45.3
15	Minneapolis–St. Paul, MN/WI	2,969	2,539	16.9
16	Cleveland–Akron, OH	2,945	2,860	3.0
17	San Diego, CA	2,813	2,498	12.6
18	St. Louis, MO/IL	2,603	2,493	4.5
19	Denver–Boulder–Greeley, CO	2,581	1,980	30.4
20	San Juan–Caguas–Arecibo, PR	2,450	2,271	7.9
21	Tampa–St.Petersburg–Clearwater, FL	2,396	2,068	15.9
22	Pittsburgh, PA	2,359	2,395	-1.5
23	Portland–Salem, OR/WA	2,265	1,793	26.3
24	Cincinnati–Hamilton, OH/KY/IN	1,979	1,818	8.9
25	Sacramento–Yolo, CA	1,797	1,481	21.3
26	Kansas City, MO/KS	1,776	1,583	12.2
27	Milwaukee–Racine, WI	1,690	1,607	5.1
28	Orlando, FL	1,645	1,224	34.3
29	Indianapolis, IN	1,607	1,380	16.4
30	San Antonio, TX	1,592	1,324	20.
31	Norfolk–Virginia Beach–Newport News, VA/NC	1,570	1,443	8.8
32	Las Vegas, NV/AZ	1,563	853	83.3
33	Columbus, OH	1,540	1,345	14.5

Source: *US Census Bureau Website*
URL: <http://www.census.gov/population/cen2000/phc-t3/tab03.pdf> Last indexed Jan. 26, 2006

The primary measure of urbanization used nowadays in the United States is not the differentiation between urban and rural, but between metropolitan and non-metropolitan areas. The latter category combines small cities and towns and the remainder of the country outside of the metropolitan areas. Statistics from 1950 onwards indicate that in the 1950s and 1960s, and again in the 1980s, metro growth rates far exceeded those of non-metropolitan areas. These were also periods of further human consolidation, and a concomitant concentration of economic wealth and power. All the same, in the 1970s, probably for the first time non-metropolitan growth exceeded that of metropolitan America. Widely described as one of de-urbanization or counter-urbanization (Berry, 1976), this period has been taken as evidence of a rural revival. The trend, however, proved short-lived and may have been in part a statistical artefact arising from the failure to extend MSA boundaries during this time.

The hierarchy of the urban system illustrates well the importance, if not the dominance, of particular metropolitan areas. Space does not permit a comprehensive list, but Table 5.5 above provides a simple ranking of the thirty-three largest MSAs and CMSAs in 1990 and again in 2000. The two factors that stand out are the massive human size of these agglomerations, and the extreme variability of growth rates. A number of the largest urban regions (2000 population greater than 2.5 million)—particularly those in Arizona, Texas and Florida, along with Atlanta (Georgia) and Denver (Colorado)—grew by 25 to 45 percent in each of the last decades of the twentieth century. Although not uncommon in the developing world, such high growth rates for metropolitan areas are seldom found elsewhere in the developed world. Clearly, urban growth has been not only brisk but highly variable over time, as well as regionally focused. The whys, wheres, and consequences of this uneven pattern warrant further examination.

The transformation of the population of urban America may be viewed as the combined outcome of three principal controlling factors: natural population increase, internal or domestic migration, and international immigration. The United States, like many other countries, experienced a massive baby-boom after the Second World War, particularly from 1948 to 1963, when the birth rate rose dramatically, the average age at first marriage and birth of first child dropped, and death rates declined. The resulting population-boom, especially of young families, fueled the rapid growth of the consumer economy and the demand for jobs, new housing and social services. Another consequence was the accelerating rate of suburbanization, aided by the automobile and the highway, and by the greatly enhanced personal mobility they afforded. This huge cohort of baby-boomers still sends shock waves through the housing and labor markets, and will continue to do so for at least the first decade of this millennium. Its effects are and will be further accentuated by the sharp drop in birth and marriage rates (baby-bust) in the late 1960s and 1970s.

With the decline and then stabilization of natural population growth, internal migration and international immigration have become important determinants of the uneven pattern of urban and regional development. Some 18 percent of urban Americans change their place of residence in any particular year, and over a period of five years almost 50 percent. Roughly half of these relocate from one urban area to another. This is in no small measure due to the impact on economic growth associated with the Eisenhower Interstate System. With a highly mobile population and very high levels of internal migration, the potential for a continuing redistribution of population and economic activity remains very high.

All the same, an even more significant component of social change in urban America is international immigration. Aside from the indigenous peoples, the United States has always been a nation of immigrants, having accepted around 61 million since 1820, with over 18 million arriving since 1960. Although the rate of immigration was highest early in the twentieth century, and lowest during the Great Depression and the Second World War, in recent decades it has picked up once again, with the annual *legal* admittance of over a million in the last years.

Two characteristics of these recent immigration flows make their impacts on urban America even more significant than in the past. First of all, there has been a shift in the source countries for immigrants, leading to a major rearrangement of their ethno-cultural characteristics. Historically, almost all newcomers to the United States used to arrive from Europe, all the way until the mid-1960s when their number still remained above 50 percent. After 1965, both as a result of US immigration policy decisions and the improved economic opportunities in Europe, the sources of international immigrants to the United States shifted. In the last three decades of the century less than 15 percent of immigrants came from Europe, while almost 50 percent were from elsewhere in the Americas and more than 35 percent from Africa and Asia. These very different flows, in turn, have transformed the cultural, ethnic and racial make-up of the cities receiving the immigrants.

A second relevant feature is that the flows of international arrivals are much more spatially uneven than those of internal migrants. Modern immigration tends to be intensely concentrated geographically, focusing on only a few gateway cities. During the 1980s, for example, almost 60 percent of all immigrants settled in just five metropolitan areas: New York, Los Angeles, San Francisco, Miami and Boston. The two largest (New York and Los Angeles) alone received over 40 percent. Since most immigrants tend to follow the same paths and choose the same destinations as earlier newcomers from the same country (chain migration), these gateways acted as a magnet for immigrants not only because of diverse job opportunities but also their heterogeneous populations. As a result of this extreme concentration, the gateway metropolitan areas have taken on a demeanor very different from other conurbations as well as from those parts of the country that receive few, if any, immigrants.

The scale and complexity of the changes in the economy, demography, governance, and living environments in the American urban system defy simple generalizations and easy explanations. As a result, some form of periodization of the last fifty years of urban evolution has usually been advanced to aid interpretation. Such periods, in turn, are often linked to regional shifts in both population and economic activity. Following Borchert's "Futures of American Cities" (1991), we can distinguish three such periods covering the years from 1950 to the late 1980s, with a fourth extending from the 1990s onward. The first of these modern periods, up to the end of the 1960s, is probably best described as one of swelling urban growth and concentration. During this phase metropolitan areas grew at faster rates than non-metropolitan areas, and larger metropolitan areas grew more rapidly than smaller ones, while all this time populations in agricultural communities continued to decline. This was also a time of rapid urban growth almost everywhere in the country, reflecting the effects of the post-war baby-boom, high levels of immigration, rising incomes, and the expansion of employment in almost all sectors of the economy.

The second period, extending roughly from the early 1970s to the early 1980s, was a time of population de-concentration and a non-metropolitan (or rural) revival at the national level. The revival of small towns and rural areas, reflected in a reversal of net migration flows which had previously favored metropolitan areas, has been attributed to sundry factors, including changes in lifestyles and attitudes about where and how to live. For example, the growth rate of the North (the Northeast and Midwest regions) declined sharply to slightly more than 2 percent in the decade of 1970–80. Nationwide, the growth of large metropolitan areas dropped to scarcely more than 8 percent, well below the 15.5 percent of smaller metropolitan areas, and even the 14.3 percent of non-metropolitan areas (Frey and Speare, 1992).

This reversal, which was widely, though erroneously, construed as ushering in a post-urban era, was likely the result of several factors acting in concert. Among them were declining rates of natural growth, an ageing population, and widespread economic restructuring—notably the loss of jobs in the manufacturing sector of the economy. The older metropolitan areas in the Northeast Manufacturing Belt, such as Detroit, Pittsburgh, Cleveland, and Chicago, suffered the most from this process of de-industrialization, also losing out in the competition for expanding industries and services. At the same time, the explosion in the prices of resources such as oil, and the expansion of retirement and lifestyle migrations, favored cities in non-manufacturing regions, especially in the South and West. During this period, more than 50 percent of American population growth took place in only three states: California, Texas, and Florida.

The 1980s ushered in a third phase which featured a modest metropolitan revival and a renewed concentration of growth in the metropolitan areas. Much as they did two decades earlier, large metropolitan areas grew more rapidly (at 12.1 percent) than either the smaller metropolitan areas (10.8 percent), or the non-metropolitan areas (3.9 percent). This time round, however, the prevailing economic and social conditions differed sharply from the 1960s. Though undoubtedly complex, they were due to the severe decline in resource prices, which acted as a brake on growth in many metropolitan areas in the western states. Manufacturing, on the other hand, enjoyed a modest resurgence, though with few new jobs. Finally, the financial services and cultural industries expanded, especially in the metro areas at the top of the urban hierarchy—prominently in New York City. Other directions of growth, such as in retirement and life style migrations, almost certainly also had a hand in this reversal.

Given the complexity of these trends, there is a tendency to describe such uneven shifts in terminology designed to bring out the contrasts between different parts of the country that vie for primacy in development. It has become common, for instance, to encounter references to the Sunbelt *versus* Frostbelt/Snowbelt or, in even more flamboyant terms, differentiations of the older northern Manufacturing Belt (now often derided as the "Rustbelt") with the Sun-and-Gun Belts of the southern and western states. While it is true that metropolitan areas in the South and West have grown faster than those in the North and Midwest for several decades, it would undoubtedly be an over-simplification to categorize all places by region as a means of explaining shifts in urban populations.

If we are to identify the gainers and losers in these recent growth patterns, it helps to examine the economic bases for differential metropolitan growth (Mills and McDonald, 1994). When metropolitan areas are classified according to their dominant sector of employment or their economic base, population growth for the decades from 1970 to 1990 reveals huge differences in economic performance among seven different functional categories (Frey and Speare, 1992). The fastest-growing areas, more than 45 percent in 1980–90, tend to be resort communities, serving recreational and retirement functions. They are followed by government and military centers, with growth at 17.5 percent; medical and educational centers with more than 12 percent; and economies supported mainly by business and financial services with 14.5 percent. Strikingly, manufacturing centers grew hardly at all (1.5 percent in 1980–90), and resource-extraction communities actually declined in population over the decade (–2.4 percent). The contrast is most apparent between metropolitan areas associated with the lifestyle-and-service economy and those dependent on older manufacturing and extracting activities. Many of the new growth areas do not even owe it to the private market, with at least four of the fastest growing economies based largely on the public sector.

The trends further suggest that there is as much variability in urban growth rates *within* the above functional categories, as there is *between* them. Older, specialized manufacturing centers in the Northeast and Midwest, for example, have generally not fared well. Yet other manufacturing centers, typically those which have a stake in the new "sunrise industries" in select niche markets, including computers, transport, communications, and other high-tech industries, have done better. Those places, however, tend to be smaller, and tend to have more diversified economies which are, in turn, often linked to the presence of government agencies, research institutions, universities and colleges. Furthermore, most are located outside the traditional Manufacturing Belt, the obvious examples being Seattle, the Silicon Valley (part of the San Francisco–Oakland–San Jose metropolitan area), Salt Lake City, Austin and Atlanta.

Still others have benefited from the massive expansion in recreational (Las Vegas), entertainment (Orlando) and retirement (West Palm Beach–Boca Raton) enterprises. For example, Las Vegas MA recorded a staggering 83 percent growth rate between 1990 and 2000 (Table 5.5), by far the highest of any major metropolitan area. In the same decade, the Orlando metropolitan area also posted a considerable 34 percent growth, and West Palm Beach–Boca Raton 31 percent. Others have prospered as a consequence of association with the government (Washington, DC), the medical sector (Minneapolis/St Paul), or with sectors that play a vital role in the so-called knowledge economy, targeting education and research (Boston).

Almost all of the fastest growing and declining MAs are relatively small in size, have an enormous range in growth rates, and divide rather neatly into two functional groups. The booming communities tend to be in the South and West—notably in California, Florida, Texas and Arizona—and for the most part boast economies based either on retirement, recreation, entertainment and other leisure pursuits, or on local-service provision. The majority are also located in regions with high amenity levels and warmer climates, as well as generally lower living and production costs. The shrinking communities, on the other hand, are either industrial (Flint, Michigan), primary resource-based (Huntington, West Virginia), or agricultural service centers (Davenport, Iowa).

Among the larger metropolitan areas, those with the most robust economies tend to be closely linked on the one hand to the new service economy, and on the other to the global economic system (Kresl, 1995; Wilson, 1997). Typically they specialize in business services, most often functioning as financial capital centers, the most obvious (global) examples of which are New York and Los Angeles, and to a lesser degree Chicago, Dallas and San Francisco. These metropolitan areas increasingly play the role of command centers of their respective economies and urban systems, in addition to being principal conduits for exchanges with overseas markets and corporations. The degree of control exerted by these metropolises is a reflection of greater levels of corporate concentration, both of which in turn increase global interdependence and the growth of financial markets and related services. These trends provide evidence of escalation of wealth and power in a few metropolitan areas, especially in terms of high-order financial and business service roles, in contradistinction to the pervasive de-centralization of manufacturing and other lower-order economic functions to newer regions and smaller metropolitan areas.

The Structure and Dynamics of Modern American Cities

Having traced the evolution of the urban system, we are now well poised to examine the structural characteristics of contemporary metropolitan areas and their continually changing dynamics. At the time of this writing, more than 80 percent of Americans live in metropolitan areas, the outcome, as we have seen, of social and geographical processes firmly established by mid-twentieth century. However, within this metropolitan matrix, a notable number of great cities and many lesser ones have, in a demographic sense, declined in the wake of burgeoning suburban population growth. Around half of the US population lives in the suburbs and within the dominant metropolitan centers, with residents in the outer city outnumbering those in the center by roughly three to two. Although all these metropolitan systems are characterized by an unbelievable and increasing complexity, and although a staggering amount of variation among them makes generalizations hazardous, such generalizations are essential if we are to account for, or even convey, this complexity.

The internal structure of the American city reflects the same mixture of forces, especially transportation technology, that shaped the national urban system. This growth process has been conceptualized into a four-stage model that identifies four eras of intra-urban structural evolution (Adams, 1970). Stage I, the *Walking-Horsecar Era*, occurred prior to 1888, the year when the electric streetcar was invented. The city of this stage was a compact pedestrian environment in which everything was within a 30-minute walk, a layout only slightly augmented when horse-drawn trolleys began to operate after 1850. Stage II, the *Electric Streetcar Era*, covers roughly the period from 1888 to 1920, during which the higher speeds of the electric streetcar enabled the 30-minute travel radius, and thus the urbanized area, to swell considerably along new outlying trolley corridors. In the older core city, the central business district (CBD), as well as industrial and residential land uses, began to differentiate into their modern forms. The electric streetcar, which introduced mass transit that every city dweller could afford, allowed the heterogeneous, immigrant-dominated city population to sort itself into ethnically uniform neighborhoods.

Stage III, the *Recreational Automobile Era*, began with the initial impact of automobiles and highways in 1920 that steadily improved the accessibility of the outer metropolitan ring, thereby launching a wave of mass suburbanization that further extended the urban frontier. During this period, the still dominant central city experienced its economic peak accompanied by the partitioning of its residential space into neighborhoods sharply defined by income, ethnicity, and race. When immigration was drastically curtailed in the 1920s, industrial managers zeroed in on the large African American population of the rural South who were increasingly unemployed as the cotton-related agricultural economy fell into decline. They began to recruit these workers by the thousands, with a dramatic impact on the social geography of the industrial cities, insofar as whites were unwilling to share their living space with the racially different newcomers. The result was involuntary segregation, channeling new migrants into geographically separate, mostly inner-city, all-black areas. By the 1950s, these trends produced large and swiftly expanding ghettos, further hastening the departure of many white central-city communities and reinforcing the drift into a racially divided urban society.

Stage IV, the *Freeway Era*, has been underway since around the mid-1950s and has seen the full impact of automobiles as the primary transportation mode. The metropolis was turned inside out as expressways pushed suburban development to distances up to fifty kilometers from the central business district. In addition, the huge suburban component of the inter-urban residential mosaic, which became home to the metropolis's more affluent residents, received a massive infusion of non-residential functions, as a consequence of which it was transformed into a fully developed outer or edge city (Garreau, 1991). As the ties to the central city loosened, the outer city's growing independence was accelerated by the rise of new suburban nuclei, particularly near freeway interchanges, to serve the new local economies. These multi-purpose "activity nodes" often coalesced around large regional shopping centers whose prestigious image attracted industrial parks, office complexes, high-rise residential developments, hotels, restaurants, entertainment facilities, and even major league sports stadiums and arenas, all of which combined into a burgeoning suburban downtown—the automobile-age version of the CBD.

The rise of the edge city has produced a multi-centered metropolis consisting of the traditional CBD, as well as a collection of increasingly co-equal suburban centers, each serving a discrete and self-sufficient surrounding area. Predictably enough, the position of the central city within this new multi-nodal metropolis often suffered. No longer the dominant center for goods and services, the central business district increasingly catered to the less affluent residents of the inner city and the commuters working downtown. During the same period, manufacturing jobs also took a beating, even as many large cities adapted successfully by shifting toward the service sector. Accompanying this switch has been downtown commercial re-vitalization, frequently hand-in-hand with new construction. Residential re-investment also occurred in many sectors but this usually required the displacement of established lower-income residents, sparking bitter conflict and resentment. Beyond the CBD, however, the inner city of today remains a problem-ridden domain of low- and moderate-income dwellers, most of whom are forced to reside in ghettos from which few ever escape.

To analyze the social geography of American cities, researchers used to examine large data sets covering a range of socio-economic, educational, demographic, racial/ethnic and housing variables. These complex geographies were usually summarized in terms of three basic constructs: social class or socio-economic status, stage in the life cycle, and ethnic or racial segregation. Later research tended to emphasize both greater and smaller scale complexities, set amid larger societal changes taking place in family and household and lifestyle structures, and greater disparities in wealth and income. This has certainly been the case in the last two decades during which market hegemony has been a countervailing force to the redistribution programs associated with state welfare. Nevertheless, the above three constructs have remained remarkably durable.

Recent decades have seen a considerable amount of commentary about the increasing levels of inequality and disparity within American urban areas. The matter is made more complex by the difficulties in comparing data, and scholarly debate over the interpretation of statistics computed from various databases continues. Many studies indicate that there has been a significant rise in income inequality from the mid-1970s onwards. Moreover, analysis of 1970 data indicates income disparity between central cities and metro areas as a whole. Although later urban studies tend to go beyond the rather arbitrary central city-suburban distinction, the results suggest that these income differentials and attendant socio-geographical polarization have generally been expected to worsen.

With the middle of the income base shrinking, with many lower-wage workers (especially males) thrown on the industrial scrap-heap, with the incomes of the managerial and skilled professionals growing more rapidly than the norm, de-industrialization has been blamed for the greater income differentials within cities. And yet studies in a number of world cities, such as New York, Chicago and Los Angeles, have also demonstrated greater polarization. It is true that numerous new jobs have been created in the rapidly expanding service sector, to the point that service employment now dominates many (if not most) metropolitan labor markets. However, a lion's share of them typically pay low wages and have a high proportion of part-time employment, and as a result fail to provide job-related benefits. The restructuring of the urban labor market also contributes to disparity from the top-side down, given the many well-paid professionals in the managerial levels of the service sector, especially where knowledge-based and information-handling skills are highly rewarded financially.

Still, despite the widespread use of terms like "de-industrialized," "information-age," "post-industrial," and the like, it would be a serious blunder to conclude that American cities are in perilous industrial decline. Structural decay associated with declining industrial landscapes definitely does exist, but there are also areas of industrial growth. In general, manufacturing-based metropolitan areas have done poorly, and some substantially less than poorly. All the same, considerable industrial growth took place in those metropolitan areas such as Los Angeles and Phoenix that have diverse economies and growing populations, and hence markets for industrial products (especially consumer durables). Other places where growth has not stalled are where new kinds of industries have taken root: Los Angeles again, the Silicon Valley in central California, or the Research Triangle in the Raleigh-Durham area of North Carolina.

In terms of the internal structure and the location of manufacturing, the overall role of the given area within the metropolitan-based national system also has to be borne in mind. Places like Detroit, which have less economic diversity than most agglomerations of its size, have indeed experienced industrial decline both in the inner city and in those parts of inner suburbs where the first large-scale industrial plants were built. As a result, the city with over a million people accounts for only 20 percent of the metropolitan area's production jobs. Yet manufacturing has prospered in the outer suburbs, so that almost a third of manufacturing employment is now located there, the remainder being in the inner suburbs. Overall, however, industrial production in the Detroit MA has contracted more than any other sector of the economy (Pollard and Storper, 1996).

It might be possible to defend such a spatial re-distribution of manufacturing plants and changes in employment, the latter reflecting gains in productivity, on market-based efficiency grounds. However, in the case of Detroit, Cleveland, and numerous other cities, this particular economic geography inevitably combines with the geography of race. As a consequence, the large minority populations of these cities are spatially and thus economically disconnected from manufacturing jobs in the inner, and even more so in the distant, suburbs. A study by Kodras (1997) painted a startling picture of the overall increase in poverty in Detroit. In the face of massive industrial decline, a disproportionate burden is carried by the African-American population with a 1990 poverty rate of 35 percent, compared to 22 percent for whites. Even more alarming is that fully half of the city's black children were found to be living in poverty.

In small- or medium-sized industrial cities, such as Akron, Ohio and Syracuse, New York, where manufacturing employment has systematically declined, the general pattern is one of plant closure and job shedding in the suburbs, simply because most production has long since abandoned central city locations. Repeating the same spatial mismatch on an even smaller scale, these processes lead to inexorable economic plight for many central city workers (or potential workers), who are either unable to find jobs in the generally low-paid service economy or are insufficiently prepared for jobs in an increasingly knowledge-based economy.

Accompanying the explosive growth of service-related employment as well as new forms of industrial production has been a change in the form and landscape of American cities. The decline of central business districts, the source of much academic and social commentary in the 1970s and 1980s, has been arrested in some cases. For example, there has been a massive re-investment in CBDs to produce a new generation of structures for the information-rich activities associated with the command-and-control functions played by principal metropolitan areas in the national, continental and world economies. For some who work among striking new office towers and dramatically new skylines, inner-city living has indeed become a viable option to the long commute on crowded trains or highways from the outlying suburbs. This has assisted the twin processes of gentrification and condominium redevelopment in the inner-city neighborhoods. Nevertheless, while the amount of office-floor space in core locations has indeed risen in absolute terms, the equally rapid growth of office space in outer-city locations has meant that the core's *relative* importance in the metropolitan matrix has actually dwindled.

Office- and information-based economy has generally been of less importance in smaller towns and cities. As a result it has usually been more difficult to revive their downtown cores. Most CBDs have now completely forfeited their major retail function to suburban malls, and only niche or specialty retailing remains, sometimes tied to entertainment or recreational activities in the district. Cities with a regional-service function, which may be home to centrally located, large-scale health and educational institutions, have a much better chance to create a somewhat viable core, even if it will never regain its prominence of a bygone era. Declining industrial centers lacking these roles and facilities are, of course, at greatest risk of developing eroding and under-invested cores.

In the outer city, the most widely found forms of urban development are so-called "edge cities" (often associated with major freeway intersections), regional and super-regional malls, and defended or gated suburban communities. The mini-CBDs in the outer city were first identified in the early 1980s, and leapt into national prominence with the publication of Joel Garreau's 1991 *Edge City*. Their basic attributes include several million square feet (250,000 m^2) of office space, between a half and a million square feet (46,000 to 92,000 m^2) of retail floor space in a mall-type environment, adjacent residential development at a higher density than the typical suburban subdivisions (including a mix of apartments and townhouses), and almost total reliance on automobiles for local travel. The development of these massive complexes is for the most part the result of private sector initiative, including the planning of new communities. Two of its most widely cited examples are Irvine, in the sprawling southern California agglomeration, and Reston, in the metropolitan area of Washington, DC.

The most remarkable change in commercial land use in the last fifty years is the emergence of planned suburban shopping malls. An ever-increasing amount of retail and service business is carried out in these centers which are totally geared to the automobile for customer access. As a result, much more acreage is devoted to parking spaces than to shopping areas. Planned shopping malls grew from about one hundred in 1950 to a total of nearly 40,000 in 2000, although the pace of new construction has slowed somewhat in recent years. Although only about 10 percent are enclosed and climate-controlled, the great majority of the larger centers boast these features.

They are enclosed under a single massive roof, high enough to accommodate three or four levels of walkway and escalator-connected stores, clustered around one or more spacious atria containing fountains, waterfalls, rest areas, and other attractions for the weary shopper. The largest enclosed mega-mall is the Mall of America in Bloomington, a suburb of Minneapolis, which has 4.2 million square feet (380,000 m^2) of retail space, more than five hundred stores, an indoor theme park, and an aquarium. Prior to the 9–11 attacks on New York City, it claimed to have 40 million visitors a year, making it the leading destination in the United States, ahead of Disney World in Orlando, Graceland in Memphis, and the Grand Canyon in Arizona—combined!

Four other notable trends in commercial/retail, suburban land use are the mini-mall, the "big box" discount center, the factory-outlet complex, and the travel center. First appearing in the 1970s in the wake of the oil crisis, mini-malls are generally small, L-shaped corner buildings of five to fifteen retail outlets fronted by a small parking lot. With vacancy rates increasing and rents dropping, they may have run their course by the mid-1990s when new construction virtually came to a halt. Big-box discount centers, which experienced phenomenal growth from the 1980s onward, are enormous, high-roofed, barn-like structures. Surrounded by acres of parking spaces they basically function as discount warehouses. Some, such as Wal-Mart, the leading retailer in the world, sell general merchandise; others, like Home Depot, deal in specialized market sectors. With a lot of emphasis on volume purchasing, almost all make use of modern technological innovations in the distribution of goods, computerized tracking systems, and inventory controls.

The presence of thousands of these "big boxes" in retail business has often had fatal consequences for smaller, less efficient stores in their trade area by attracting customers away from them. Despite the harmful effects of these mega-stores on small businesses, not to mention increased traffic and air pollution, they remain sought after by urban administrators because of the windfall in sales taxes. This may be changing, however, with signs of a surging political backlash in communities who seek to exclude these giants in order to protect local small retailers. Factory-outlet centers consist of from ten to fifty specialized stores, each selling merchandise from a single, well-known, branded line. They are usually located next to a freeway in the outer suburbs to permit easy access by a large market of shoppers. Also located in the outer suburbs are the newest developments, travel centers. These huge truck stops cover several acres, with most of the area given over to parking for trucks and semi-trailers. The focal point is a restaurant or café, but there are also gasoline retailing facilities, mini-markets, garage facilities and sometimes motel accommodations.

The gated community, or defended suburb, is widely seen as the ultimate expression of the individual ideology of Americans—the right to erect a wall to keep those who don't belong out. In reality it is a deliberate withdrawal from the metropolitan community and an abdication of personal responsibility for its social condition. It is also a mirror on the extraordinary level of concern many Americans have about violence and crime. Defended suburbs are, after all, a practical if draconian way to insulate oneself and one's family from the real or perceived threat that permeates daily life in the Big Bad City (after the 1999 eponymous novel by America's foremost urban and crime proceduralist, Ed McBain). Still, gated communities are home to a relatively small number of people compared to the vast legions of suburbanites who continue to live "in the open." Of course, many of the latter share the same concerns that impel individuals and families who move into defended compounds. However, most feel reasonably secure in exclusive housing compounds concealed from easy viewing from the road, which have road layouts deliberately designed to confuse the casual visitor with nefarious purposes in mind. Tellingly, personal security systems with private guards or police who respond on activation are now standard suburban equipment.

The Future of Urbs Americana

Since the American city is a "work in progress," the time has come to peer into the crystal ball in search of the future in which new forces will mold and transform the metropolis of the twenty- first century. Despite the hazards of overgeneralization, we may assert with some confidence that American cities largely grew into their present prominence as a result of a global industrialization led by the manufacturing sector. However, the common use today of terms such as "post-industrial" or "information-age" when considering urbanization suggests that a dramatic global transformation is underway. Indeed, some urbanists now blame economic globalization and the polarizing of the emergent transnational capitalist class and its low-wage labor force for such recent urban patterns as gentrification, immigrant ghetto expansion, and the marginalization of the poor. We might thus expect to find manifestations of this rapid economic change as the American metropolis evolves into the City of the Future.

Several interrelated issues are likely to affect the fates of the nation's cities. First, the ongoing effects of de-industrialization and the dismantling of social programs has already dramatically increased the gap between rich and poor. Next, the lack of clear and consistent federal policy towards cities has left many municipalities struggling to come up with solutions to issues that are fundamentally national in character. Finally, new immigrants continue to reshape urban ethnic and racial communities, unsettling prior political alliances and creating new forms of urban culture.

More than half a decade into the new century, what do these trends spell for the future geography of urbanization in America, for the patterns of foreseeable growth, and for the ongoing reorganization of the urban systems? If there is one thing of which we can be certain, it is that the dynamics of population change and urban economic growth are likely to remain as volatile as ever. Whether the trends and patterns described earlier will continue into the first decades of the twenty-first century, or whether a new urban era will ensue, is not yet so clear. With lower rates of national population growth, it is plausible that the processes that influence the redistribution of population and economic activity within the urban system will assume a more important role in shaping the future of the American city.

A host of factors contribute to the uncertainty that inevitably accompanies any attempt to predict some future state of a sufficiently complex system. In the context of the American city, among the most significant are an aging population, international immigration and ethnic pluralism, major shifts in lifestyles and consumer preferences, economic restructuring, technological innovation, trade liberalization and global economic competition. By 2010 the proportion of the population aged over sixty-five will reach 22 percent of the national total. This is the time when the oldest members of the massive baby-boom of the immediate postwar years reach retirement age. Legitimately, a futurologist may ask a series of related questions, such as: Where will this huge population live? Will they continue to reside in their present locations? The vast majority now live in the older and larger metropolitan areas. Will they migrate to smaller cities and towns in less expensive and/or amenity-rich areas?

An additonal issue is immigration from abroad. Unless specific policy decisions curtail it, this important dimension will probably continue to have critical, and unevenly distributed, repercussions for select metropolitan areas. The most obvious impact will be on cities that serve as primary destinations or gateways for immigrants. These will certainly be transformed, at least in their social structure, perhaps largely in positive ways but still not without social tensions. Some of the bigger metropolitan areas, such as Los Angeles, San Francisco, New York, and Miami, already have populations that are now over 40 percent foreign-born. Since most other parts of the country, except along the Mexico border, receive few immigrants, a clear differentiation is beginning to emerge between these gateway cities and the rest. Indeed, the debate rages on as to whether overseas immigrants are replacing or displacing native-born populations, and in so doing leading to a "balkanization" of American metropolitan areas (Frey, 1995; Frey and Liaw, 1998).

Balkanization—a geopolitical term coined during the armed conflicts in Europe's Balkan region in the 20th century—originally described fragmentation into smaller, often hostile or non-cooperative, areas. In our context, it intimates the spatial fragmentation (ghettoization) arising when immigrants with different overseas origins flock to and settle in metropolitan areas. Interestingly, in the recent years there have been attempts to use the term in a positive way, by equating it with the need for sustenance of a particular community or identity. Its usage in relation to the immigrant issue is also valid in this sense. Without exception, all of the bigger metropolitan areas mentioned above have recorded big losses in terms of net internal migration, while attracting large numbers of foreign migrants.

Continuing economic restructuring, involving a progressive global economic integration arising from trade-liberalization policies and trans-border flows, as well as the hyper-mobility of modern global financial markets, further adds to the uncertainty of prognosis. What we can say is that the places that are likely to benefit most from "freer" trade and globalization are the same places that have benefited from shifts in national and regional economies over the last two decades, notably urban areas in the southern and western states. Cities with high-tech industries or high-order service and financial functions, as well as those with high retirement, recreation and entertainment utility and educational and health-related economies, are also well placed to do well in this environment. Those with low-wage economies, rusting industries, a limited range of services and few environmental amenities, and those poorly located with respect to the overall geography of the American urban system, will likely lose out most from intensified competition.

The consequence of these powerful forces will be that American cities will continue gradually to evolve in directions established over the last half century, but with more regional variation than up to now. The urban hierarchy will continue to shift gradually to the South and West, but again with a more intricate organization than in the past. The largest twenty metropolitan areas listed in Table 5.5 will still continue to dominate, but with population and power shifting to the newer metropolitan areas, notably Los Angeles, San Francisco, Dallas, Houston, Miami and Atlanta, and to an even larger number of soon-to-be very large metropolitan areas, such as Phoenix, Tampa-St. Petersburg, Orlando, Seattle, and Denver.

The scale of urban growth and the long-term implications of creating such colossal metropolitan agglomerations should not be underestimated. Consider the following scenario, based on existing demographic trends, put forward plausibly by Borchert (1991). By the second decade of the 21st century, the emergent megalopolitan structure in the United States will be dominated by a massive sprawl in southern California, stretching from Santa Barbara to Los Angeles and San Diego, and relegating the New York–New Jersey–Long Island metropolitan region to second place. Similarly, the San Francisco–Oakland–San Jose–Sacramento conurbation will probably pass the Chicago–Gary–Milwaukee region, moving into third place. Other super-conurbations, such as an emerging central Florida metropolis (Tampa–Orlando–Daytona Beach), and the existing south Florida metropolis (Miami–West Palm Beach), will also move up the urban hierarchy. Although the population figures which Borchert posited for these super-conurbations are now well short of what will be the case, the critical question is how does one even come to terms with such massive agglomerations of people and infrastructure, let alone manage them?

Is it likely that the continued expansion of the knowledge economy and the electronically wired world of telecommunication and the Internet will stop, or even reverse, the tendency towards spatial concentration? An alternative scenario arises in response to the question. The construction of the network of commerce and communication (the information superhighway) has transformed business and economic activities in ways that could not have been foreseen only a few years ago. Today high technology companies like Cisco, Intel, and Microsoft are household names, in correlation with the continued rise in the power and prestige of highly sophisticated users of technology by, for example, Amazon, Dell, Fed-Ex, and Wal-Mart. In theory, these kinds of innovations make everyone and everywhere in the national economic system easily and equally accessible. Still lacking however, is a high speed pipeline into most American homes. In the 3rd quarter of 2005, the household penetration rate for Internet broadband was just over 33 percent, compared with over 73 percent for Hong Kong and over 67 percent for South Korea (WebSiteOptimization.com, 2006).

There is little doubt that an increasing number of routine economic functions will be physically decentralized to smaller communities and peripheral areas, transferred overseas, or revamped into online operations. Yet, at the same time, one must not overlook the nature of the telecommunications industry, the lag in the penetration of broadband, and the aspirations of most individuals in terms of where and with whom they want to live and work. These almost ensure a continued escalation and concentration of high-order services, information-intense functions, and jobs in large metropolitan command centers—especially those already rich in amenities and cultural activities.

The most obvious, and probably the most reliable, generalization about the American urban system is that there will be even more of the same. However, it seems that the patterns of growth and their associated problems will be considerably more complex and more spatially variable than what we've seen in the past. Today the American city remains what it has always been: a center of economic, social and cultural opportunity. The outlook, though it may seem daunting and foreboding, is nevertheless not bereft of hope. Better planning, neighborhood political activism, and creative leadership can fuel inner-city revival as demonstrated in places as widely diverse as Baltimore, San Antonio, and Seattle. A continuing challenge for citizens and policy makers alike, however, is how to reduce the negative consequences of the uneven profile of growth and prosperity, and how to alleviate the inevitable disparities in the quality of urban life for all citizens.

Notes

Chapter 1   **All Roads Lead from the American City?**

1. Lind, "Red-state sneer," 28.
2. Monkkonen, *America Becomes Urban*, 69.
3. Monkkonen, 74.
4. Chudacoff and Smith, *The Evolution of American Urban Society*, 5.
5. Thomas Jefferson to James Madison, December 20, 1787, in *The Papers of Thomas Jefferson*, 12:442.
6. Jefferson to John Adams, 1813, in *The Writings of Thomas Jefferson: Memorial Edition*, 13:401.
7. Jefferson, *Notes on Virginia* Q. XIX, 1782, in *ibid.*, 2:230.
8. Jefferson to David Williams, November 14, 1803, in *ibid.*, 10:431.
9. Longworth, *Austin and Mabel*.
10. Chudacoff and Smith, 115.
11. Fox, *Metropolitan America*, 24.
12. Higham, *Send These to Me*, 22.
13. Chudacoff and Smith, 116–8.
14. Chambers, *The Tyranny of Change*, 41–2, 99–103; Rafferty, *Apostle of Human Progress;* Fox, *The Discovery of Abundance;* White, *Social Thought in America;* Strout, *The Pragmatic Revolt in American History;* Rader, *The Academic Mind and Reform;* Crunden, *Ministers of Reform;* Feffer, *The Chicago Pragmatists and American Progressivism;* Fink, *Progressive Intellectuals and the Dilemmas of Democratic Commitment;* Fried, *The Progressive Assault on Laissez Faire;* Noble, *The Progressive Mind, 1890–1917.*
15. Rodgers, *Atlantic Crossings;* Kloppenberg, *Uncertain Victory.*
16. Fry and Kurz, *Washington Gladden;* Curtis, *A Consuming Faith;* Gorrell, *The Age of Social Responsibility;* Hopkins, *The Rise of the Social Gospel;* Handy, ed., *The Social Gospel in America.*

17. See Chudacoff and Smith, 187–90; Carson, *Settlement Folk*; Davis, *Spearheads for Reform*; Davis, *American Heroine*; Linn, *Jane Addams*; Elshtain, *Jane Addams*; Sklar, *Florence Kelley*; Daniels, *Always a Sister*; Stivers, *Bureau Men, Settlement Women*.

18. For figures, see Monkkonen, 69–73; on the announcement, Chudacoff and Smith, 203.

19. Chudacoff and Smith, 203; Wrobel, *The End of American Exceptionalism*, esp. chs. 1–5; on Turner and the frontier thesis, see also Bogue, *Frederick Jackson Turner*; Jacobs, *The Historical World of Frederick Jackson Turner*; Hofstadter, *The Progressive Historians*; Jacobs, *On Turner's Trail*.

20. Fox, 6.

21. Chudacoff and Smith, 147–8.

22. Strauss, *Images of the American City*, 171–8.

23. William Jennings Bryan, "Cross of Gold" speech, July 9, 1896, in Reid, 606.

24. McCullough, *Mornings on Horseback*, ch. 15; Morris, *The Rise of Theodore Roosevelt*, ch. 11; Brands, *T. R.*, chs. 7–8; Dalton, *Theodore Roosevelt*, 97–104; White, *The Eastern Establishment and the Western Experience*.

25. Quoted in Brands, 173–4.

26. Roosevelt, *The Rough Riders*; also Heatley, ed., *Bully!*

27. Cutright, *Theodore Roosevelt*; Nash, *Wilderness and the American Mind*, 149–53.

28. Roosevelt, "Race Decadence," 1911, reprinted in Dinunzio, ed., *Theodore Roosevelt*, 339–43; Dyer, *Theodore Roosevelt and the Idea of Race*, 143–67.

29. Higham, *Strangers in the Land*, 136–44, 175–82; Anderson, *Race and Rapprochement*, 54–7, 81–2.

30. Quotations from Roberts, "Willard Straight," 505.

31. Finnegan, *Against the Specter of a Dragon*, 106–14; Pearlman, *To Make Democracy Safe for America*, 124–33, 150–4; Clifford, *The Citizen Soldiers*, 195–203.

32. Salmond, *The Civilian Conservation Corps*.

33. Chudacoff and Smith, 227–8; Lubell, *The Future of American Politics*, 34–41.

34. Lubell, 54–5.

35. Monkkonen, 70.

36. Fox, 24.

37. Monkkonen, 72–3.

38. Heilbrun, *Hamlet's Mother and Other Women*, 92.

39. Monkkonen, 74–5.

40. See, e.g., Chudacoff and Smith, 126–35; Burns, *The Workshop of Democracy*, 136–42.

41. Monkkonen, ch. 4.

42. Steffens, *The Shame of the Cities*; Chudacoff and Smith, 152–66; Brogan, *The Pelican History of the United States of America*, 409–12.

43. Burns, ch. 7; McKelvey, *The Emergence of Metropolitan America 1915–1966*, 1–2; Chudacoff and Smith, 166–201; Monkkonen, ch. 5; also Dahl, *Who Governs?*

44. de Tocqueville, *Democracy in America*, 512.

45. Quoted in Chudacoff and Smith, 145.

46. Chudacoff and Smith, 146.

47. Chudacoff and Smith, 88–108; Fox, 40–1; Jackson, *Crabgrass Frontier*, chs. 4–10.

48. Teaford, *City and Suburbs*, ch. 2.

49. McKelvey, 16; Chudacoff and Smith, 117.

50. McKelvey, 16–7.
51. McKelvey, 20–3; Chudacoff and Smith, 222–6.
52. Jackson, *The Ku Klux Klan in the City*; Lay, ed., *The Invisible Empire in the West*; MacLean, *Behind the Mask of Chivalry*.
53. Chudacoff and Smith, 204; McKelvey, 22–3, 38–9.
54. Chudacoff and Smith, 208–15; Monkkonen, 167–81.
55. Chudacoff and Smith, 208–15; Monkkonen, 167–81; Jackson, *Crabgrass Frontier*, chs. 13, 15.
56. Chudacoff and Smith, 215; Fox, 34–8.
57. McKelvey, 123–5; Chafe, *The Unfinished Journey*, 20.
58. Chudacoff and Smith, 236–40, 249–59; McKelvey, 174–87.
59. Jackson, *Crabgrass Frontier*, ch. 14; Chafe, 118–9; Fox, 103–4; Kay, *Asphalt Nation*, ch. 10.
60. Mills, *White Collar*; Whyte, *The Organization Man*; Riesman et al., *The Lonely Crowd*.
61. Chafe, 141–2.
62. Chudacoff and Smith, 259–76.
63. On the growth of the sunbelt cities, see Abbott, *The New Urban America*; Kirkpatrick, *Power Shift*; Wiley and Gottlieb, *Empires in the Sun;* Markusen, Hall, Campbell, and Deitrick, *The Rise of the Gunbelt*; Nash, *World War II and the West*.
64. Steinbeck, *The Grapes of Wrath*. The figures are taken from Monkkonen, 85–7; on California's experience of urbanization and industrial development in this period, see Starr's works, *Endangered Dreams*; *The Dream Endures*; and *Embattled Dreams*; on California's earlier history, see his *Americans and the California Dream*; *Inventing the Dream*; and *Material Dreams*.
65. Chudacoff and Smith, 274–5.
66. Chudacoff and Smith, 272–4, 277–80; Chafe, esp. chs. 12–16; Miles, *The Odyssey of the American Right*, chs. 12–17; Brennan, *Turning Right in the Sixties*; Hodgson, *The World Turned Rightside Up*; Ferguson and Rogers, *Right Turn*.
67. Dean, *Imperial Brotherhood*, esp. ch. 7.
68. Slotkin, *Gunfighter Nation*.
69. On Reagan, see Reagan, *An American Life*; Pemberton, *Exit with Honor*; Jeffords, *Hard Bodies*; White, *The New Politics of Old Values*; Blumenthal, *Our Long National Daydream*; Schaller, *Reckoning with Reagan;* Mervin, *Ronald Reagan and the American Presidency*. On George W. Bush, see Lind, *Made in Texas*; Minutaglio, *First Son*; Gregg and Rozell, eds., *Considering the Bush Presidency*; Fred I. Greenstein, ed., *The George W. Bush Presidency*; Campbell and. Rockman, eds., *The Bush Presidency*.
70. Judt, "Europe vs. America," 37–41.
71. Kagan, "Power and Weakness," 3; later expanded as Kagan, *Of Paradise and Power*, 3.
72. Potter, *People of Plenty*.

Chapter 2 In the City and on the Road in Asian American Film

1. My thanks to Peter Swirski for his helpful suggestions and to Renee Tajima-Peña for permission to use stills from *My America*.
2. See Slethaug (2001).
3. Christine Choy is also the principal cinematographer on *My America*. The film won the 1997 award for best cinematography at Sundance.

4   For more on the film and its relationship to Tajima-Peña's oeuvre, see Gateward (1999) and Leong (1998). For ideas on using *My America* and other Asian American films in the classroom, see Marchetti (2006).

5.   See Okihiro (1994).

6.   For more on Asian Americans and the politics of race in the United States, see Lowe (1996) and Palumbo-Liu (1999).

7.   All dates related to Asian American history in this chapter are taken from Asian American History Timeline, *Ancestors in the Americas.*

8.   On the role of the 442nd in World War II, see Loni Ding's *The Color of Honor* (1988).

9.   On the Japanese in Chicago, see *Chicago Japanese American Historical Society (CJAHS): Census 2000 Portrait of Japanese Americans in Metropolitan Chicago.*

10. For an investigation of the impact of the Los Angeles violence on Korean Americans, see Dai Sil Kim-Gibson and Christine Choy's *Sa-I-Gu* (1993).

11. For more on the road movie, see Laderman (2002); Cohan and Hark (1997).

12. For a full treatment of the city film, see Clark (1997).

13. Feng (2002) provides a discussion of the film and the search for Asian American identity.

14. In fact, Wong had an impressive film career with appearances in *Nightsongs* (1984), *Year of the Dragon* (1985), *Dim Sum* (1985), *Big Trouble in Little China* (1986), *The Last Emperor* (1987), *3 Ninjas* (1992), *The Joy Luck Club* (1993), and *Seven Years in Tibet* (1997), among others.

15. For more on miscegenation and its depiction in American popular culture, see Marchetti (1993 and 2001).

16. Another documentary portrait of Yuri Kochiyama can be found in Rea Tajiri, *Yuri Kochiyama: A Passion for Justice* (1999).

17. Asian American cinema boasts many fine films on the injustice of the Internment and its impact on the lives of Japanese Americans, including *Family Gathering* (Lise Yasui, 1988), *History and Memory* (Rea Tajiri, 1991), *Manzanar* (Robert Nakamura, 1971), *Memories from the Department of Amnesia* (Janet Tanaka, 1991), *Rabbit in the Moon* (Emiko Omori, 1999), *Strawberry Fields* (Rea Tajiri, 1997), and *Days of Waiting* (Steven Okazaki, 1988).

18. For another view of the Laotian community in the Midwest, see Taggart Siegel's *Blue Collar and Buddha* (1988).

Chapter 3   A Is for American, B Is for Bad, C Is for City

1.   For a distinction and discussion of apocalyptic and integrated scholarship, see Eco, *Apocalypse Postponed* (1994), and Swirski, *From Lowbrow to Nobrow* (2005). The material in the first two sections also appears in Swirski, "The Novels of Ed McBain and the Politics of the American *Polis*" (2006).

2.   For a comprehensive analysis of *Playback*, see Chapter 5, "Raymond Chandler's Aesthetics of Irony," in Swirski, *From Lowbrow to Nobrow.*

3.   Inspector Morse was played to perfection by the late John Thaw in the hit television series. Dexter put Morse to rest in *The Remorseful Day*, the last novel of the cycle.

4.   Liukkonen, "Maj Sjowall (1935–)."

5. The combined figures for the US, Canada, Great Britain, Australia, New Zealand and South Africa were: 1952: 14 hits; 1962: 57 hits; 1972: 214 hits; 1982: 1,092 hits; 1,992: 4,230 hits; and 2002: 7,952 hits. While again demonstrably on the low side, the statistics document the dazzling expansion of crime fiction. For US sales figures, see Book Industry Study Group.

6. Blum et al., 474.

7. Cited in Blum et al., 470.

8. Cited in Panek, 4.

9. Cited in Panek, 5.

10. See Rasula for a superb analysis of the comics wars in the 1950s.

11. See Swirski and Wong (2006), and Panek (1990) for background.

12. Raab, 13.

13. Both quotes in this paragraph from *Cop Hater*, xiv.

14 For a full analysis of *Playback*, see Swirski, *From Lowbrow to Nobrow* (2005), Chapter 5. I would like to thank Faye Wong for her help with the following sections.

15. Raab, 13. For web access, see, <http://users.bestweb.net/~foosie/mcbain.htm>.

16. National Center for Health Statistics, Table 131 (page 1), "No Health Insurance Coverage Among Persons Under 65 Years of Age According to Selected Characteristics: United States, selected years 1984–2002."

17. See Raab (the introductory section).

18. Page 82; also, table: "Unemployment Rates for Selected Groups in the Labour Force: 1947 to 1998" in *Datapedia*, 86.

19. Raab, 13.

20. Hunt, 174.

21. See Australasian Council of Women and Policing Inc.

22. Cited in Carr, 15.

23. For detailed analysis of the contemporary legal procedural, see Swirski and Wong (2006).

Chapter 4 *Just Apassin' Through*

1. According to the 2003 National Hospital Ambulatory Survey, 44,065 Americans lost their lives in auto-related accidents. In 2002, an average of 16.6 persons per 100,000 had injuries that eventually led to their deaths (tables 29, 30, 44, 84); see McCaig and Burt (2005).

2. See Zsoldost (2006).

3. See Gillam. The poem is also available at <http://www.egyptology.com/extreme/mehy>.

4. See Waugh, *Dissonant Worlds* (1996).

5. Quoted in Aptheker, 20.

6. The Hopewell and Adena Trails are only two examples of this kind of absorption; see <http://www.rosscountyparkdistrict.com/map.htm>.

7. Hatch and Stout, 40.

8. *The Works, Vol. 10*, 226. Following quote from *The Works, Vol. 14*, 72.

9. Sermon, March 1737, 31; reprinted in McDermott, 20.

10. On these issues, see Brauer (1976); and Hughey (1983).

11. See Swirski and Reddall (2003).
12. In Bush, 90.
13. In Barck and Lefler, 362.
14. Barck and Lefler, 256.
15. As Daniel Boone had been hired to do; for more on this subject, see Carroll, 7.
16. In Blake, 274.
17. See especially pages 20–3.
18. The infamous St. Valentine's Day Massacre is still a visitor's site on the "Haunted Chicago" tour of the city. For background and data on the homeless, see National Coalition for the Homeless: Report.
19. I have valued the sage advice of architect James Triscott in this section.
20. For more on this interpretation of Pynchon's novel, see Ostrander, 124.

Bibliography

Introduction American City or Global Village?

Diamond, Jared. *Collapse: How Societies Choose to Fail or Succeed.* London: Penguin, 2005.

Fox, Justin. "The Great Paving: How the Interstate Highway System Helped Create the Modern Economy—and Reshaped the FORTUNE 500." *Fortune* 149:1 (26 January, 2004): 77–84.

Loewy, Raymond F. In ePodunk. "Quotes." 2006. <http://www.epodunk.com/quotes/ny1.html>. Indexed March 1, 2006.

Wolfe, Thomas. *The Web and the Rock.* New York: Harper and Row, 1986 (Orig. 1939).

Chapter 1 All Roads Lead from the American City?

Abbott, Carl. *The New Urban America: Growth and Politics in Sunbelt Cities.* Chapel Hill: University of North Carolina Press, 1981.

Anderson, Stuart. *Race and Rapprochement: Anglo-Saxonism and Anglo-American Relations, 1895–1904.* Rutherford, NJ: Fairleigh Dickinson UP, 1981.

Blumenthal, Sidney. *Our Long National Daydream: The Political Pageant of the Reagan Era.* New York: HarperCollins, 1988.

Bogue, Allan G. *Frederick Jackson Turner: Strange Roads Going Down.* Norman: University of Oklahoma Press, 1998.

Brands, H. W. *T. R.: The Last Romantic.* New York: Basic Books, 1997.

Brennan, Mary C. *Turning Right in the Sixties: The Conservative Capture of the GOP.* Chapel Hill: University of North Carolina Press, 1995.

Brogan, Hugh. *The Pelican History of the United States of America.* New York: Viking Penguin, 1986.

Burns, James MacGregor. *The Workshop of Democracy: From the Emancipation Proclamation to the Era of the New Deal.* New York: Vintage Books, 1986.

Campbell, Colin, and Bert A. Rockman, eds. *The Bush Presidency: Appraisals and Prospects.* Washington, DC: Congressional Quarterly Press, 2003.

Carson, Mina. *Settlement Folk: Social Thought and the American Settlement Movement, 1885–1930.* Chicago: University of Chicago Press, 1990.

Chafe, William H. *The Unfinished Journey: America Since World War II.* 4th ed. New York: Oxford UP, 1999.

Chambers, John Whiteclay, II. *The Tyranny of Change: America in the Progressive Era, 1900–1920.* 2nd ed. New Brunswick, NJ: Rutgers UP, 2000.

Chudacoff, Howard P., and Judith E. Smith. *The Evolution of American Urban Society.* 6th ed. Upper Saddle River, NJ: Pearson Prentice Hall, 2005.

Clifford, John Garry. *The Citizen Soldiers: The Plattsburg Training Camp Movement, 1913–1920.* Lexington: University of Kentucky Press, 1972.

Crunden, Robert M. *Ministers of Reform: The Progressives' Achievement in American Civilization, 1889–1920.* New York: Basic, 1982.

Curtis, Susan. *A Consuming Faith: The Social Gospel and Modern American Culture.* Columbia: University of Missouri Press, 2001.

Cutright, Paul Russell. *Theodore Roosevelt: The Making of a Conservationist.* Urbana: University of Illinois Press, 1985.

Dahl, Robert A. *Who Governs? Democracy and Power in an American City.* New Haven: Yale UP, 1961.

Dalton, Kathleen. *Theodore Roosevelt: A Strenuous Life.* New York: Alfred A. Knopf, 2002.

Daniels, Doris Groshen. *Always a Sister: The Feminism of Lillian D. Wald.* New York: Feminist Press, 1989.

Davis, Allen F. *Spearheads for Reform: The Social Settlements and the Progressive Movement, 1890–1914.* New Brunswick, NJ: Rutgers UP, 1984.

——. *American Heroine: The Life and Legend of Jane Addams.* Chicago: Ivan R. Dee, 2000.

Dean, Robert D. *Imperial Brotherhood: Gender and the Making of Cold War Foreign Policy.* Amherst: University of Massachusetts Press, 2001.

DiNunzio, Mario R., ed. *Theodore Roosevelt: An American Mind: Selected Writings.* New York: Viking Penguin, 1994.

Dyer, Thomas G. *Theodore Roosevelt and the Idea of Race.* Baton Rouge: Louisiana State UP, 1980.

Elshtain, Jean Bethke. *Jane Addams and the Dream of American Democracy: A Life.* New York: Basic, 2002.

Feffer, Andrew. *The Chicago Pragmatists and American Progressivism.* Ithaca, NY: Cornell UP, 1993.

Ferguson, Thomas, and Joel Rogers. *Right Turn: The Decline of the Democrats and the Future of American Politics.* New York: Hill and Wang, 1986.

Fink, Leon. *Progressive Intellectuals and the Dilemmas of Democratic Commitment.* Cambridge: Harvard UP, 1997.

Finnegan, John Patrick. *Against the Specter of a Dragon: The Campaign for American Military Preparedness, 1914–1917.* Westport, CT: Greenwood, 1974.

Fried, Barbara H. *The Progressive Assault on Laissez Faire: Robert Hale and the First Law and Economics Movement.* Cambridge: Harvard UP, 1998.

Fox, Daniel M. *The Discovery of Abundance: Simon N. Patten and the Transformation of American Social Theory.* Ithaca, NY: Cornell UP, 1967.

Fox, Kenneth. *Metropolitan America: Urban Life and Urban Policy in the United States, 1940–1980.* London: Macmillan, 1985.

Fry, C. George, and Joel R. Kurz. *Washington Gladden as a Preacher of the Social Gospel, 1882–1918.* Lewiston, NY: Edwin Mellen Press, 2003.

Gorrell, Donald K. *The Age of Social Responsibility: The Social Gospel in the Progressive Era, 1900–1920.* Macon, GA: Mercer UP, 1988.

Greenstein, Fred I., ed. *The George W. Bush Presidency: An Early Assessment.* Baltimore, MD: Johns Hopkins UP, 2003.

Gregg, Gary L., and Mark J. Rozell, ed. *Considering the Bush Presidency.* New York: Oxford UP, 2003.

Handy, Robert T., ed. *The Social Gospel in America, 1870–1920.* New York: Oxford UP, 1966.

Heatley, Jeff, ed. *Bully! Colonel Theodore Roosevelt, the Rough Riders and Camp Witkoff, Montauk, New York 1898: A Newspaper Chronicle with Roosevelt's Letters.* Montauk, NY: Montauk Historical Society and Pushcart Press, 1998.

Heilbrun, Carolyn G. *Hamlet's Mother and Other Women.* New York: Columbia UP, 1990.

Higham, John. *Send These to Me: Immigrants in Urban America.* Revised ed. Baltimore, MD: Johns Hopkins UP, 1984.

——. *Strangers in the Land: Patterns of American Nativism 1860–1925.* 2nd ed. New York: Atheneum, 1971.

Hodgson, Godfrey. *The World Turned Rightside Up: The Conservative Ascendancy in America.* Boston: Houghton Mifflin, 1996.

Hofstadter, Richard. *The Progressive Historians: Turner, Beard, Parrington.* New York: Knopf, 1968.

Hopkins, Charles Howard. *The Rise of the Social Gospel in American Protestantism, 1865–1915.* New York: AMS Press, 1982 (Orig. 1940).

Jacobs, Wilbur R. *The Historical World of Frederick Jackson Turner: With Selections From His Correspondence.* New Haven: Yale UP, 1968.

——. *On Turner's Trail: 100 Years of Writing Western History.* Lawrence: University Press of Kansas, 1994.

Jackson, Kenneth T. *Crabgrass Frontier: The Suburbanization of the United States.* New York: Oxford UP, 1985.

Jackson, Kenneth T. *The Ku Klux Klan in the City, 1915–1930.* New York: Oxford UP, 1967.

Jefferson, Thomas. *The Papers of Thomas Jefferson.* Eds. Julian P. Boyd et al. 33 vols. to date. Princeton: Princeton UP, 1950–.

——. *The Writings of Thomas Jefferson: Memorial Edition.* Eds. Andrew A. Lipscomb and Albert E. Bergh. 20 vols. Washington, DC: Thomas Jefferson Memorial Association, 1903–1904.

Jeffords, Susan. *Hard Bodies: Hollywood Masculinity in the Reagan Era.* New Brunswick, NJ: Rutgers UP, 1994.

Judt, Tony. "Europe vs. America." *New York Review of Books* 52:2 (February 10, 2005): 37–41.

Kagan, Robert. "Power and Weakness." *Policy Review* 113:3 (2002): 3–28.

——. *Of Paradise and Power: America and Europe in the New World Order.* New York: Knopf, 2003.

Kay, Jane Holt. *Asphalt Nation: How the Automobile Took Over America and How We Can Take It Back.* New York: Crown Publishers, 1997.

Kirkpatrick, Sale. *Power Shift: The Rise of the Southern Rim and Its Challenge to the Eastern Establishment.* New York: Random House, 1975.

Kloppenberg, James T. *Uncertain Victory: Social Democracy and Progressivism in European and American Thought, 1870–1920.* New York: Oxford UP, 1986.

Lay, Shawn, ed. *The Invisible Empire in the West: Toward a New Appraisal of the Ku Klux Klan in the 1920s.* Urbana: University of Illinois Press, 1992.

Lind, Michael. *Made in Texas: George W. Bush and the Southern Takeover of American Politics.* New York: Basic, 2003.

——. "Red-state sneer." *Prospect* 106 (2005): 26–31.

——. *Vietnam, The Necessary War: A Reinterpretation of America's Most Disastrous Military Conflict.* New York: Basic, 1999.

Linn, James Weber. *Jane Addams: A Biography.* Urbana, IL: University of Illinois Press, 2000.

Longworth, Polly. *Austin and Mabel: The Amherst Affair and the Love Letters of Austin Dickinson and Mabel Loomis Todd.* New York: Farrar Straus Giroux, 1994.

Lubell, Samuel. *The Future of American Politics.* New York: Harper & Brothers, 1952.

MacLean, Nancy. *Behind the Mask of Chivalry: The Making of the Second Ku Klux Klan.* New York: Oxford UP, 1994.

Markusen, Ann, et al. *The Rise of the Gunbelt: The Military Remapping of Industrial America.* New York: Oxford UP, 1991.

McCullough, David. *Mornings on Horseback.* New York: Simon and Schuster, 1981.

McKelvey, Blake. *The Emergence of Metropolitan America 1915–1966.* New Brunswick, NJ: Rutgers UP, 1968.

Mervin, David. *Ronald Reagan and the American Presidency.* London: Longman, 1990.

Miles, Michael W. *The Odyssey of the American Right.* New York: Oxford UP, 1980.

Mills, C. Wright. *White Collar: The American Middle Classes.* New York: Oxford UP, 1951.

Minutaglio, Bill. *First Son: George W. Bush and the Bush Family Dynasty.* New York: Crown Books, 1999.

Monkkonen, Eric H. *America Becomes Urban: The Development of U.S. Cities & Towns 1780–1980.* Berkeley: University of California Press, 1988.

Morris, Edmund. *The Rise of Theodore Roosevelt.* New York: Random House, 1979.

Nash, Gerald D. *World War II and the West: Reshaping the Economy.* Lincoln: University of Nebraska Press, 1990.

Nash, Roderick Frazier. *Wilderness and the American Mind.* 4th ed. New Haven: Yale UP, 2001.

Noble, David W. *The Progressive Mind, 1890–1917.* Revised ed. Minneapolis, MN: Burgess Publishing, 1981.

Pearlman, Michael. *To Make Democracy Safe for America: Patricians and Preparedness in the Progressive Era.* Urbana: University of Illinois Press, 1984.

Pemberton, William E. *Exit with Honor: The Life and Presidency of Ronald Reagan.* Armonk, NY: M. E. Sharpe, 1998.

Potter, David. *People of Plenty: Economic Abundance and the American Character.* Chicago: Phoenix Books, 1954.

Rader, Benjamin G. *The Academic Mind and Reform: The Influence of Richard T. Ely in American Life.* Lexington: University Press of Kentucky, 1966.

Rafferty, Edward C. *Apostle of Human Progress: Lester Frank Ward and American Political Thought, 1841–1913.* Lanham, MD: Rowman and Littlefield, 2003.

Reagan, Ronald. *An American Life.* New York: Simon and Schuster, 1990.

Reid, Ronald F., ed. *Three Centuries of American Rhetorical Discourse.* Prospect Heights, IL: Waveland Press, 1988.

Riesman, David, et al. *The Lonely Crowd: A Study of the Changing American Character.* Garden City, NY: Doubleday, 1956.

Roberts, Priscilla. "Willard Straight, The First World War, and 'Internationalism of All Sorts': The Inconsistencies of an American Liberal Interventionist." *Australian Journal of Politics and History* 44:4 (1998): 493–511.

Rodgers, Daniel T. *Atlantic Crossings: Social Politics in a Progressive Age.* Cambridge, MA: Belknap Press, 1998.

Roosevelt, Theodore. *The Rough Riders.* New York: Scribner's, 1899.

Salmond, John A. *The Civilian Conservation Corps, 1933–1942: A New Deal Case Study.* Durham, NC: Duke UP, 1967.

Schaller, Michael. *Reckoning With Reagan: America and Its President in the 1980s.* New York: Oxford UP, 1992.

Sklar, Kathryn. *Florence Kelley and the Nation's Work.* New Haven: Yale UP, 1995.

Slotkin, Richard. *Gunfighter Nation: The Myth of the Frontier in Twentieth-Century America.* New York: Atheneum, 1992.

Starr, Kevin. *Americans and the California Dream 1850–1915.* New York: Oxford UP, 1986.

———. *Coast of Dreams: California on the Edge, 1990–2003.* New York: Knopf, 2004.

———. *The Dream Endures: California Enters the 1940s.* New York: Oxford UP, 1997.

———. *Embattled Dreams: California in War and Peace, 1940–1950.* New York: Oxford UP, 2002.

———. *Endangered Dreams: The Great Depression in California.* New York: Oxford UP, 1996.

———. *Inventing the Dream: California Through the Progressive Era.* New York: Oxford UP, 1985.

———. *Material Dreams: California Through the 1920s.* New York: Oxford UP, 1990.

Steffens, Lincoln. *The Shame of the Cities.* New York: Hill and Wang, 1992 (Orig. 1904).

Steinbeck, John. *The Grapes of Wrath.* New York: The Modern Library, 1939.

Stivers, Camilla. *Bureau Men, Settlement Women: Constructing Public Administration in the Progressive Era.* Lawrence: University Press of Kansas, 2000.

Strauss, Anselm L. *Images of the American City.* New York: Free Press of Glencoe, 1961.

Strout, Cushing. *The Pragmatic Revolt in American History: Carl Becker and Charles Beard.* Westport, CT: Greenwood Press, 1958.

Teaford, Jon C. *City and Suburbs: The Political Fragmentation of Metropolitan America, 1850–1970.* Baltimore, MD: Johns Hopkins UP, 1979.

de Tocqueville, Alexis. *Democracy in America.* Eds. Harvey C. Mansfield and Delba Winthrop. Chicago: University of Chicago Press, 2000.

White, G. Edward. *The Eastern Establishment and the Western Experience: The West of Edward Remington, Theodore Roosevelt, and Owen Wister.* New Haven: Yale UP, 1968.

White, John Kenneth. *The New Politics of Old Values.* 2nd ed. Hanover, NH: University of New England Press, 1990.

White, Morton. *Social Thought in America: The Revolt Against Formalism.* New York: Oxford UP, 1976.

Whyte, William H. *The Organization Man.* New York: Simon and Schuster, 1955.

Wiley, Peter, and Robert Gottlieb. *Empires in the Sun: The Rise of the New American West.* Tucson: University of Arizona Press, 1982.

Wrobel, David M. *The End of American Exceptionalism: Frontier Anxiety from the Old West to the New Deal.* Lawrence: University Press of Kansas, 1993.

Chapter 2   In the City and on the Road in Asian American Film

Asian American History Timeline. *Ancestors in the Americas.* 1998. <http://www.cetel.org/timeline.html>. Indexed February 2, 2006.

Chicago Japanese American Historical Society: (CJAHS): Census 2000 Portrait of Japanese Americans in Metropolitan Chicago. 2006. <http://www.cjahs.org/CJAHSDiscoverNikkeiCensus2000.pdf>. Indexed February 2, 2006.

Clark, David B., ed. *The Cinematic City.* London: Routledge, 1997.

Cohan, Steven, and Ina Rae Hark, eds. *The Road Movie Book.* London: Routledge, 1997.

Feng, Peter X. *Identities in Motion: Asian American Film and Video.* Durham, NC: Duke UP, 2002.

Gateward, Frances. "Rediscovering Asian America." *Angles* 4:1 (1999): 9–11.

Hamamoto, Darrell, and Sandra Liu, eds. *Countervisions: Asian American Film Criticism.* Philadelphia: Temple UP, 2001.

Laderman, David. *Driving Visions: Exploring the Road Movie.* Austin: University of Texas Press, 2002.

Leong, Russell. "Film Review: *My America … or Honk if You Love Buddha.*" *Journal of Asian American Studies* 1: 1 (February 1998): 117–9.

Lowe, Lisa. *Immigrant Acts: On Asian American Cultural Politics.* Durham, NC: Duke UP, 1996.

Marchetti, Gina. "America's Asia: Hollywood's Construction, Deconstruction, and Reconstruction of the 'Orient.'" In Garcia, Roger, *Out of the Shadows: Asians in American Cinema.* Milan: Edizioni Olivares, produced in conjunction with the 54th Locarno International Film Festival, 2001. 37–57.

——. "Using Film and Video to Teach about Asians and Asian Americans Across the Curriculum." In Gerster, Carole, with Laura W. Zlogar, ed., *Teaching Ethnic Diversity with Film: Essays and Resources for Educators in History, Social Studies, Literature and Film Studies.* Jefferson, NC: McFarland and Company, 2006. 41–57.

——. *Romance and the "Yellow Peril": Race, Sex, and Discursive Strategies in Hollywood Fiction.* Berkeley: University of California Press, 1993.

Okihiro, Gary Y. *Margins and Mainstreams: Asians in American History.* Seattle: University of Washington Press, 1994.

Palumbo-Liu, David. *Asian/American: Historical Crossings of a Racial Frontier.* Palo Alto, CA: Stanford UP, 1999.

Slethaug, Gordon E. "The Exotic and Oriental as Decoy: Raymond Chandler's *The Big Sleep.*" In Luk, Thomas Y. T., and James P. Rice, eds., *Before and After Suzie: Hong Kong in Western Film and Literature.* Hong Kong: The Chinese University of Hong Kong, 2001. 161–84.

Tajima-Peña, Renee. "Interview." Mozaik Features. *Urban Mozaik Magazine* (2000). <http://urbanmozaik.com/member_fea_archives/01mar_arc_fea_myamerica.html>. Indexed February 2, 2006.

Tajima-Peña, Renee. "No Mo Po Mo and Other Tales of the Road." In Hamamoto, Darrell, and Sandra Liu, eds., *Countervisions: Asian American Film Criticism.* Philadelphia: Temple UP, 2001. 245–62.

Chapter 3   A Is for American, B Is for Bad, C Is for City

Ashley, Mike. *The Mammoth Encyclopedia of Modern Crime Fiction.* New York: Carroll & Graf, 2002.

Australasian Council of Women and Policing Inc. "2002 Women and Policing Globally." 2002. <http://www.auspol-women.asn.au/3rd_conf_Monday_AM.htm>. Indexed January 2, 2006.

Blum, John M. et al. *The National Experience: A History of the United States.* Fort Worth: Harcourt Brace Jovanovich, 1981.

Book Industry Study Group, et al. "Romance Industry Statistics." <http://www. rhondawoodward.com/pdf/PK1102IndustryStats.pdf>. Indexed January 2, 2006.

Bourne, Larry S., ed. *Internal Structure of the City: Readings on Space and Environment.* New York: Oxford UP, 1971.

Bowker's Global Books in Print. 2004. <http://www.globalbooksinprint.com>. Indexed June 11, 2005.

Carr, John C. *The Craft of Crime: Conversations with Crime Writers.* Boston: Houghton Mifflin, 1983.

Davis, Mike. *The Ecology of Fear: Los Angeles and the Imagination of Disaster.* New York: Vintage, 1999.

Dexter, Colin. *The Remorseful Day.* London: Pan, 1999.

Eco, Umberto. *Apocalypse Postponed.* Ed. Robert Lumley. Bloomington: Indiana UP, 1994.

Grant, Percy Stickney. "Are the Rich Responsible for New York's Vice and Crime?" *Everybody's Magazine* 5:27 (1901): 555–60.

Hahn Rafter, Nicole. *Encyclopedia of Women and Crime.* Phoenix: Oryx Press, 2000.

Herbert, David T., and Colin J. Thomas. *Cities in Space: City as Place.* London: David Fulton, 1990.

Hong Kong Government. "A Summary of Crime Situation in 2002." 2002. <http://www. info.gov.hk/info/crime/02crime-e.htm>. Indexed January 2, 2006.

Hoover, J. Edgar. *Crime in the United States: the Uniform Crime Report—1963.* Boston: Beacon, 1965.

Hubin, Allen J. *Crime Fiction II: A Comprehensive Bibliography 1749–1900.* New York, London: Garland, 1994.

Hunt, Jennifer C. "Police Subculture and Gender." In Hahn Rafter, Nicole, *Encyclopedia of Women and Crime.* Phoenix: Oryx Press, 2000.

Kipling, Rudyard. *American Notes.* London, New York: Standard Book Company, 1930 (Orig. 1891).

Kurian, George Thomas, ed. *Datapedia of the United States 1790–2005: America Year by Year.* 2nd ed. Lanham, MD: Bernan Associates, 2000.

Liukkonen, Petri. "Maj Sjowall (1935–)." 2000. <http://www.kirjasto.sci.fi/sjowall.htm>. Indexed January 2, 2006.

Marshall, William Leonard. *The Hatchet Man.* London: Hamish Hamilton, 1976.

McBain, Ed. *Fat Ollie's Book.* New York: Pocket Books, 2003.

——. *The Last Dance.* New York: Pocket Books, 2000.

——. *The Big Bad City.* New York: Pocket Books, 1999.

——. *Mischief.* New York: Pocket Books, 2003 (Orig. 1993).

——. *Kiss.* London: Mandarin, 1992.

——. *The Heckler.* New York: Pocket Books, 2003 (Orig. 1960).

——. *Give the Boys a Great Big Hand.* New York: Pocket Books, 2003 (Orig. 1960).

——. *Killer's Payoff.* New York: Pocket Books, 2003 (Orig. 1958).

——. *The Mugger.* New York: Warner, 1996 (Orig. 1956).

——. *Cop Hater.* New York: Warner, 1999 (Orig. 1956).

National Center for Health Statistics. "Health, United States, 2004." 2004. <http://www. cdc.gov/nchs/products/pubs/pubd/hus/metro.htm#healthcare>. Indexed January 2, 2006.

Meloy, Michelle L. "Police Organizations, Municipal and State." In Mukherjee, Satyanshu K., and Jocelynne A. Scutt, eds., *Women and Crime.* Sydney, Boston: Australian Institute of Technology in association with Allen & Unwin, 1981.

Olcott, Anthony. *Russian Pulp: The "Detektiv" and the Way of Russian Crime.* Lanham, MD: Rowman & Littlefield, 2001.

O'Leary Morgan, Kathleen, Scott Morgan, and Neal Quitno. *City Crime Rankings: Crime in Metropolitan America.* 3rd ed. Lawrence, KS: Morgan Quitno Press, 1997.

Panek, Leroy Lad. *Probable Cause: Crime Fiction in America.* Bowling Green, OH: Bowling Green State University Popular Press, 1990.

Raab, Selwyn. "Interview: Writing Under an Assumed Name." *New York Times* (January 30, 2000): section 7:13.

Rasula, Jed. "Nietzsche in the Nursery: Naive Classics and Surrogate Parents in Postwar American Cultural Debates." *Representations* 29 (Winter 1990): 50–77.

Reichs, Kathy. "Kathy and John Discuss their Work." 2005. <http://www.kathyreichs.com/ mybooks.htm>. Indexed January 29, 2006.

Riis, Jacob. *How the Other Half Lives: Studies Among the Tenements of New York.* In Crisci, Madeline, *Public Health in New York City in the Late Nineteenth Century.* Bethesda, MD: National Library of Medicine, History of Medicine Division, 1990 (Orig.1890).

Schumer, Charles E. "Schumer: New Federal Budget Cuts Endanger NYC Hospitals' Ability to Deal with Future Terror Attacks." December 4, 2002. <http://schumer. senate.gov/SchumerWebsite/pressroom/press_releases/PR01352.htm>. Indexed January 2, 2006.

Swirski, Peter. "The Novels of Ed McBain and the Politics of the American *Polis.*" In Chanady, Amaryll, George Handley, and Patrick Imbert, eds., *America's Worlds and the World's America.* Ottawa: University of Ottawa/Legas, 2006.

——. *From Lowbrow to Nobrow.* Montreal: McGill-Queen's UP, 2005.

——. "Popular and Highbrow Literature: A Comparative View." In Tötösy de Zepetnek, Steven, ed., *Comparative Literature and Comparative Cultural Studies.* West Lafayette: Purdue UP, 2003. 183–205. Originally in: *CLCWeb: Comparative Literature and Culture: A WWWeb Journal* 1, 1999. <http://clcwebjournal.lib.purdue.edu/clcweb99_4/ swirski99.html>.

Swirski, Peter, and Faye Wong. "Briefcases for Hire: American Hardboiled to Legal Fiction." *Journal of American Culture* 29:3 (2006): 307–20.

US Department of Justice. "Law Enforcement Statistics." 7 September, 2004. <http:// www.ojp.usdoj.gov/bjs/lawenf.htm#LEMAS>. Indexed January 2, 2006.

Walling, George Washington. *Recollections of a New York Chief of Police: An official record of thirty-eight years as a patrolman, detective, captain, inspector and chief of the New York Police.* New York: Caxton book concern, limited, 1887.

Zalesky, Jeff. "The Big Bad City." *Publishers Weekly* 245:49 (December 7, 1998): 54.

Chapter 4 *Just Apassin' Through*

Aptheker, Herbert. *The Colonial Era*. New York: International Publishers, 1974 (Orig. 1959).

Auster, Paul. *The New York Trilogy*. New York: Penguin, 1990.

Baldwin, James. *If Beale Street Could Talk*. London: Penguin Classics, 1994 (Orig. 1974).

Barck, Oscar T., Jr., and Hugh T. Lefler. *Colonial America*. New York: Macmillan, 1968.

Bataille, Georges. *Guilty*. Venice, CA: Lapis Press, 1988.

Beagle, Peter S. *I See by My Outfit*. New York: Viking, 1965.

Beeman, Richard R. *The Varieties of Political Experience in Eighteenth-Century America*. Philadelphia: University of Pennsylvania Press, 2004.

Bell, Michael. *Space Replaces Us!* Toronto: Penguin Canada, 2003.

Belloc, Hilaire. *The Road*. Manchester: C. W. Hobson, 1923.

Blake, Casey Nelson. "An Atmosphere of Effrontery: Richard Serra, *Tilted Arc*, and the Crisis of Public Art." In Fox, Richard Wightman, and T. J. Jackson Lears, eds. *The Power of Culture: Critical Essays in American History*. Chicago: University of Chicago Press, 1993. 247–89.

Blum, Alan. *The Imaginative Structure of the City*. Montreal: McGill-Queens UP, 2003.

Brauer, Jerald. "Puritanism, Revivalism, and the Revolution." In *Religion and the American Revolution*. Philadelphia: The University of Philadelphia, 1976. 18–27.

Bush, Sargent, Jr. "The Journal of Madam Knight." In Andrews, William, et al, eds. *Journeys in New Worlds: Early American Women's Narratives*. Madison: University of Wisconsin Press, 1990. 67–116.

Calvino, Italo. *Le Città Invisibili*. Turin: Einaudi, 1972.

Carroll, Michael Thomas. *Popular Modernity in America*. New York: SUNY, 2000.

DiPrima, Diane. *Memoirs of a Beatnik*. New York: Olympia, 1969.

Dreiser, Theodore. *An American Tragedy*. New York: New American Library, 1960 (Orig. 1925).

——. *A Traveller at Forty*. New York: Century Company, 1913.

——. *A Hoosier Holiday*. New York: John Lane Company, 1916.

Edmonds, Mark K. (Tiger). *Longrider: A Tale of Just Passin' Through*. Livingston, AL: Livingston Press, 1998.

——. "Literature of the American Road." 2002. <http://www.billdudley.com/litroad.html>. Indexed February 20, 2006.

Edwards, Jonathan. *The Works of Jonathan Edwards—Volume 14: Sermons and Discourses, 1723–1729*. Ed. Kenneth P. Minkema. New Haven: Yale UP, 1997.

——. *The Works of Jonathan Edwards—Volume 10: Sermons and Discourses, 1723–1729*. Ed. Wilson H. Kimnach. New Haven: Yale UP, 1992.

Emerson, Ralph Waldo. *Society and Solitude and Other Essays*. New York: Cosimo, 2005 (Orig. 1870).

Gabel, Shainee, and Kristin Hahn. *Anthem: An American Road Story*. New York: Avon, 1997.

Gillam, Robyn. "The Mehy Papers: Texts and Lifestyle in Translation." *Chronique d'Egypt* 75, fasc. 150 (2000): 205.

Ginsberg, Allan. *Howl and Other Poems*. New York: City Lights Books, 1956.

Hatch, Nathan O., and Harry S. Stout, eds. *Jonathan Edwards and the American Experience*. New York: Oxford UP, 1988.

Heat Moon, William Least. *Blue Highways: A Journey into America.* Boston: Little, Brown and Company, 1982.

Hinton, Susan E. *Rumble Fish.* New York: Bantam, 1975.

Hughey, Michael W. *Civil Religion and Moral Order: Theoretical and Historical Dimensions.* Westport, CT: Greenwood Press, 1983.

Jackson, J. B. "Other-Directed Houses." In Zube, E. H., ed. *Landscapes: Selected Writings of J.B. Jackson.* Amherst: University of Massachusetts Press, 1970. 55–72.

Jacobs, Jane. *The Death and Life of Great American Cities.* New York: Vintage, 1961.

Jones, Phyllis M., and Nicholas R. Jones, eds. *Salvation in New England.* Austin: University of Texas, 1977.

Kay, J. H. *Asphalt Nation: How the Automobile Took Over America and How We Can Take It Back.* New York: Crown Publishers, 1997.

Kaplan, Robert. *An Empire Wilderness: Travels into America's Future.* New York: Random House, 1998.

Kerouac, Jack. *On the Road.* New York: Penguin, 1991 (Orig. 1957).

Kunstler, James Howard. *The Geography of Nowhere.* New York: Simon and Schuster, 1992.

———. *The Long Emergency.* New York: Grove/Atlantic, 2005.

Laurents, Arthur, and Stephen Sondheim. *West Side Story.* New York: William Heinemann, 1957.

Lefebvre, Henri. *The Urban Revolution.* Trans. Robert Bononno. Minneapolis: University of Minnesota Press, 2003.

Mailer, Norman. *Miami and the Siege of Chicago.* New York: The World Publishing Company, 1968.

Marsden, George M. *Jonathan Edwards: A Life.* New Haven: Yale UP, 2003.

Mather, Cotton. *Days of Humiliation: Times of Affliction and Disaster.* Gainesville, FL: Scholars Facsimiles and Reprints, 1970.

———. *On the Necessities and Advantages of a Public Spirit.* Boston: Samuel Green, 1690.

McCaig, Linda F., and Catherine W. Burt. *National Hospital Ambulatory Medical Care Survey: 2003 Emergency Department Summary #358.* May 26, 2005. <http://www.cdc.gov.nchs/data/ad/ad358.pdf>. Indexed February 28, 2006.

McDermott, Gerald R. *One Holy and Happy Society: The Public Theology of Jonathan Edwards.* University Park: Pennsylvania State UP, 1992.

McInerney, Jay. *Bright Lights, Big City.* New York: Vintage, 1984.

McMurtry, Larry. *Roads: Driving America's Great Highways.* New York: Simon and Schuster, 2001.

Miller, Donald W., Jr. "Books by the Beat Generation." 2004. <http://www.donaldmiller.com>. Indexed February 20, 2006.

Miller, Perry. *Orthodoxy in Massachusetts.* Cambridge, MA: Harvard UP, 1933.

———. *New England Mind: From Colony to Province.* Cambridge, MA: Harvard UP, 1953.

———. *Errand into the Wilderness.* New York: Harper Torchbooks, 1964 (Orig. 1956).

Miller, Perry, and Thomas H. Johnston. *The Puritans.* New York: American Book Co., 1938.

Mumford, Lewis. *The Culture of Cities.* New York: Harcourt, Brace, 1938.

National Coalition for the Homeless: Report. "Hate, Violence and Death on Main Street USA—A Report on Hate Crimes and Violence against People Experiencing Homelessness in 2005." <http://www.nationalhomeless.org/getinvolved/projects/hatecrimes/index.html>. Indexed February 26, 2006.

Ostrander, Madeline. "Awakening to the Physical World: Ideological Collapse and Ecofeminist Resistance in *Vineland.*" In Abbas, Niran, ed., *Thomas Pynchon: Reading from the Margins.* Cranbury, NJ: Associated University Presses, 2003. 122–35.

Primeau, Ronald. *The Romance of the Road: The Literature of the American Highway.* Bowling Green, OH: Bowling Green State University Popular Press, 1996.

Pirsig, Robert. *Zen and the Art of Motorcycle Maintenance.* Toronto: Bantam, 1974.

Pynchon, Thomas. *Vineland.* Boston: Little, Brown, 1990.

——. *V.* London: Vintage, 1995 (Orig. 1963).

Raban, Jonathan. *Soft City.* Glasgow: Collins, 1974.

Reynolds, Frank, with Michael McClure. *Freewheelin' Frank: Secretary of the Angels.* New York: Grove Press, 1967.

Robbins, Tom. *Even Cowgirls Get the Blues.* Boston: Houghton Mifflin, 1976.

Rykwert, Joseph. *The Seduction of Place: The History and Future of Cities.* New York: Vintage, 2002.

Sommer, Robert. *Tight Places: Hard Architecture and How to Humanize It.* Englewood Cliffs, NJ: Prentice-Hall, 1974.

Steinbeck, John. *Travels with Charley in Search of America.* New York: Viking, 1962.

——. *The Grapes of Wrath.* New York: The Modern Library, 1939.

Stephenson, Gregory. *The Daybreak Boys: Essays on the Literature of the Beat Generation.* Carbondale: Southern Illinois UP, 1990.

Steppenwolf. "Born to be Wild." (1968). Lyrics by M. Bonfire.

Swirski, Peter, and David Reddall. "American Literature: Overview." *Dictionary of American History.* Vol. 5. Ed. David Hollinger. New York: Scribner's, 2003. 116–23.

Thompson, Hunter S. *Fear and Loathing in Las Vegas: A Savage Journey to the Heart of the American Dream.* New York: Random House, 1976.

Tunnard, Christopher, and Boris Pushkarev. *Man-Made America: Chaos or Control?* New Haven: Yale UP, 1963.

Waugh, Earle, H. *Dissonant Worlds: Roger Vandersteene among the Cree.* Waterloo, Ontario: Wilfrid Laurier UP, 1996.

Wolfe, Tom. *Electric Kool-Aid Acid Test.* New York: Farrar, Straus & Giroux, 1968.

——. *The Kandy-kolored Tangerine-flake Streamline Baby.* New York: Farrar, Straus & Giroux, 1965.

Zinn. Howard. *A People's History of the United States.* New York: Harper Perennial, 1995.

Zsoldost, Carolyn. "Rite of Passage: How I Got to be Cool with My First Car." *Road and Travel Magazine.* 2006. <http://www.roadandtravel.com/roadhumor/riteofpsg.html>. Indexed January 20, 2006.

Chapter 5 *Urbs Americana*

Adams, John S. "Residential Structure of Midwestern Cities." *Annals of the Association of American Geographers* 60 (1970): 37–62.

Berry, Brian J.L. *Urbanization and Counter-urbanization.* Beverly Hills, CA: Sage, 1976.

Birdsall, S. S., et al. "Megalopolis." *Regional Landscapes of the United States and Canada.* 6th ed. New York: Wiley, 2005. 61–86.

Borchert, John R. "American Metropolitan Evolution." *Geographical Review* 57 (1967): 301–32.

——. "Futures of American Cities." In Hart, John F., ed., *Our Changing Cities.* Baltimore, MD: Johns Hopkins UP, 1991. 218–50.

Chudacoff, Howard P., and Judith E. Smith. *The Evolution of American Urban Society.* 6th ed. Upper Saddle River, NJ: Prentice-Hall, 2005.

Fox, Justin. "The Great Paving: How the Interstate Highway System Helped Create the Modern Economy—And Reshaped the FORTUNE 500." *Fortune* 149:1 (26 January, 2004): 77–84.

Frey, William H. "The New Geography of Population Shifts." In Farley, Reynolds, ed., *State of the Union: America in the 1990s, Volume XI.* New York: Russell Sage Foundation, 1995. 271–334.

Frey, William H., and Kao-Lee Liaw. "Immigrant Concentration and Domestic Migrant Dispersal: Is Movement to Nonmetropolitan Areas White Flight?" *Professional Geographer* 50:2 (1998): 215–32.

Frey, William H., and Alden Speare, Jr. "The Revival of Metropolitan Growth in the US." *Population and Development Review* 18:1 (1992): 129–46.

Garreau, Joel. *Edge City: Life on the New Frontier.* New York: Doubleday, 1991.

Gibson, Campbell. "Population of the 100 Largest Cities and Other Urban Places in the United States: 1790 to 1990." June 1998. <http://www.census.gov/population/www/documentation/twps0027.html>. Indexed January 26, 2006.

Greer, Scott. *The Emerging City: Myth and Reality.* New Brunswick NJ: Transaction Publishers, 1999.

Hofstadter, Richard. "The Agrarian Myth and Commercial Realities." *The Age of Reform.* New York: Knopf, 1956. 23–59.

Jackson, Kenneth T. *Crabgrass Frontier: The Suburbanization of the United States.* New York: Oxford UP, 1985.

Kaszynski, William. *The American Highway: The History and Culture of Roads in the United States.* Jefferson, NC: McFarland, 2000.

Kodras, J. "The Changing Map of American Poverty in an Era of Economic Restructuring and Political Enlightenment." *Economic Geography* 73 (1997): 67–93.

Kresl, Peter K., ed. *North American Cities and the Global Economy.* London: Sage, 1995.

Lemon, James T. *Liberal Dreams and Nature's Limits: Great Cities of North America since 1600.* New York: Oxford UP, 1996.

McKnight, Tom L. "The North American City." *Regional Geography of the United States and Canada.* 2nd ed. Upper Saddle River, NJ: Prentice-Hall, 1997. 60–91.

Mills, Edwin S., and John F. McDonald, eds. *Sources of Metropolitan Growth.* New Brunswick, NJ: Rutgers UP, 1994.

Pollard, J., and M. Storper. "A Tale of Twelve Cities: Metropolitan Employment Change in Dynamic Industries in the 1980s." *Economic Geography* 72:1 (1996): 1–22.

Tunnard, C., and H. H. Reed. *American Skyline: The Growth and Form of our Cities and Towns.* New York: New American Library, 1956.

US Census Bureau. "Historical Metropolitan Area Definitions." June 1999. <http://www.census.gov/population/www/estimates/pastmetro.html>. Indexed January 26, 2006.

US Census Bureau. "Metropolitan Areas Ranked by Population: 2000." April 2001. <http://www.census.gov/population/cen2000/phc-t3/tab03.pdf >. Indexed January 26, 2006.

US Census Bureau. "Metropolitan Statistical Areas and Components, December 2005, with codes." January 2006. <http://www.census.gov/population/estimates/metro_general/List4.txt>. Indexed January 26, 2006.

Ward, David. *Cities and Immigrants: A Geography of Change in Nineteenth-Century America.* New York: Oxford UP, 1971.

Warner, Sam B. *The Urban Wilderness: A History of the American City.* New York: Harper & Row, 1972.

WebSiteOptimization.com. "The Bandwidth Report 0601." January 2006. <http://www.websiteoptimization.com/bw/0601/>. Indexed January 26, 2006.

Wilson, D., ed. "Globalization and the Changing US City." *Annals of the American Academy of Political and Social Science* 551 (1997). Special Issue.

Yates, Maurice. *The North American City.* 5th ed. New York: Longman, 1998.

Contributors

Priscilla Roberts received her degrees from King's College, Cambridge. Since 1984 she has taught history at the University of Hong Kong, where she is associate professor and also honorary director of the Centre of American Studies. She has published articles on twentieth-century diplomatic and international history, with a special interest in Anglo-American relations, in the *Business History Review, Journal of American Studies, Journal of American-East Asian Relations*, and other periodicals. She is the author of *The Cold War* (2000), and the editor of *Sino-American Relations Since 1900* (1991); *Window on the Forbidden City: The Beijing Diaries of David Bruce, 1973–1974* (2001); and *Behind the Bamboo Curtain: China, Vietnam, and the World Beyond Asia* (2006). She is associate editor of several encyclopedias published by ABC-CLIO, including the *Encyclopedia of the Korean War* (2000); *Encyclopedia of World War II* (2004); *World War II: A Student Encyclopedia* (2005); *Encyclopedia of World War I* (2005); *World War I: A Student Encyclopedia* (2005); and *Encyclopedia of the Cold War* (forthcoming). She is co-editor of a forthcoming volume on women and international relations. Currently she is working on a major study of the twentieth-century trans-Atlantic foreign policy establishment.

Gina Marchetti is Associate Professor at the Department of Comparative Literature, the University of Hong Kong. Previously, she was Associate Professor in the Department of Cinema and Photography at Ithaca College. In 1995 her book, *Romance and the "Yellow Peril": Race, Sex and Discursive Strategies in Hollywood Fiction*, won the award for best book in the area of cultural studies from the Association for Asian American Studies. She has published in anthologies such as *Classic Hollywood, Classic Whiteness; Keyframes: Popular Cinema and Cultural Studies; At Full Speed: Hong Kong Cinema in a Borderless World; Ladies and Gentlemen, Boys and Girls: Gender in Film at the End of the Twentieth Century; Out of the Shadows: Asians* in *American Cinema*; *Countervisions: Asian American Film Criticism*; *The Cinema of Hong Kong*; *Transnational Chinese Cinemas*; *The Birth of Whiteness: Race and the Emergence of United States Cinema*; *Unspeakable Images: Ethnicity and the American Cinema*, and others. Her current books are *From Tian'anmen to Times Square: Transnational China and the Chinese Diaspora on Global Screens*, and *Hollywood and the New Global Cinema* (co-edited with Tam See Kan).

Peter Swirski is Associate Professor of American Literature and Culture and Director of American Studies at the University of Hong Kong. His specialty is twentieth-century American literature, history, and culture, as well as interdisciplinary studies in literature, philosophy, and science. Recognized internationally as the leading Stanislaw Lem scholar, he has published more than fifty articles in professional journals and lectured in the Americas, Europe and Asia. His books are: *A Stanislaw Lem Reader* (1997); *Between Literature and Science: Poe, Lem, and Explorations in Aesthetics, the Cognitive Sciences, and Literary Knowledge* (2000); *From Lowbrow to Nobrow* (2005); *The Art and Science of Stanislaw Lem* (2006); *Of Literature and Knowledge: Explorations in Narrative Thought Experiments, Evolution, and Game Theory* (2007); and *Ars Americana, Ars Politica* (forthcoming).

Earle Waugh is Professor Emeritus of Religious Studies at the University of Alberta. Schooled at the University of Chicago under Mircea Eliade and Joseph Kitagawa, he focused his early work on Islamic Studies. This led him to explore the wide variety of expressions of that religion and culture, including those in North America. This work led, among others, to the publication of his *Diasporic Studies in North America: The Muslim Community in North America* (1983), *The Muslim Family in North America* (1991), and *The Shaping of an American Islamic Discourse* (1998). Most recently, he co-edited *Diaspora Serbs: A Cultural Analysis* (2004). Waugh has been a much sought-after commentator in the media on Muslim affairs, and has often lectured both in Canada and the United States on Islamic Affairs. His commitment to cross-cultural understanding won him the Prelorentzos Peace Award for lifelong educational activity for peace in 2004. Until recently chair of the interdisciplinary department of Comparative Literature, Religion and Film Studies, he is currently director of the Centre for the Cross-Cultural Study of Health and Healing in the University's Department of Family Medicine, as well as consultant on cultural and ethnic issues in America and beyond.

William John Kyle was born in the United Kingdom and holds a PhD in Geography from McMaster University in Canada. He is Associate Professor in the Department of Geography at the Faculty of Arts, the University of Hong Kong. His principal research interests are in the physical environment (especially the climate) and its myriad inter-relationships with human societies. Editor-in-Chief of the *Hong Kong Meteorological Society Bulletin* from 1991 to 2002, he has also served on the Editorial Board of *Asian Geographer* from 1996 to the present. Author of numerous articles in journals from the *Australian Meteorological Magazine* to *Land Use Policy*, most recently he has co-edited *Climate of China* (2007). He has taught a wide variety of courses and seminars, from "Contemporary Global Environmental Issues", "Spatial Distribution of Hazards and Disasters", "Atmospheric Environment and Global Climate", "The Geography of Wine", "Environmental Hazards, Climate Change and the Environment", to a regional geography course, "North America". Since 2000 he has been closely involved with the American Studies Program at the University of Hong Kong, teaching and co-teaching "On the Road in the American Culture" and "On the Road Again" with the American Studies director, Peter Swirski.

Index of Names